WEAPONS OF MASS DESTRUCTION

WEAPONS OF MASS DESTRUCTION

EDITED BY ROBERT CURLEY, MANAGER, SCIENCE AND TECHNOLOGY

Britannica®
Educational Publishing

IN ASSOCIATION WITH

ROSEN
EDUCATIONAL SERVICES

Published in 2012 by Britannica Educational Publishing
(a trademark of Encyclopædia Britannica, Inc.)
in association with Rosen Educational Services, LLC
29 East 21st Street, New York, NY 10010.

Distributed exclusively by Rosen Educational Services.
For a listing of additional Britannica Educational Publishing titles, call toll free (800) 237-9932.

First Edition

Britannica Educational Publishing
Michael I. Levy: Executive Editor
J.E. Luebering : Senior Manager
Adam Augustyn: Assistant Manager
Marilyn L. Barton: Senior Coordinator, Production Control
Steven Bosco: Director, Editorial Technologies
Lisa S. Braucher: Senior Producer and Data Editor
Yvette Charboneau: Senior Copy Editor
Robert Curley: **Manager, Science and Technology**

Rosen Educational Services
Shalini Saxena: Editor
Nelson Sá: Art Director
Cindy Reiman: Photography Manager
Brian Garvey: Designer
Introduction by Alexandra Hanson-Harding

Library of Congress Cataloging-in-Publication Data

Weapons of mass destruction/edited by Robert Curley.—1st ed.
    p. cm.—(The Britannica guide to war)
"In association with Britannica Educational Publishing, Rosen Educational Services."
Includes bibliographical references and index.
ISBN 978-1-61530-687-9 (library binding)
1. Weapons of mass destruction—History. 2. Arms control—History. I. Curley, Robert, 1955–
U793.W424 2012
358'.3—dc23

2011029787

Manufactured in the United States of America

On the cover: The signature mushroom cloud of a nuclear explosion can be seen after a
1970 French nuclear test in Polynesia. Islands in the South Pacific were frequently the sites
of nuclear tests for much of the 20th century. *AFP/Getty Images*

On pages 1, 19, 39, 64, 77, 92, 103, 119, 141: The sign indicating nuclear radiation.
Shutterstock.com

CONTENTS

89

107

112

INTRODUCTION

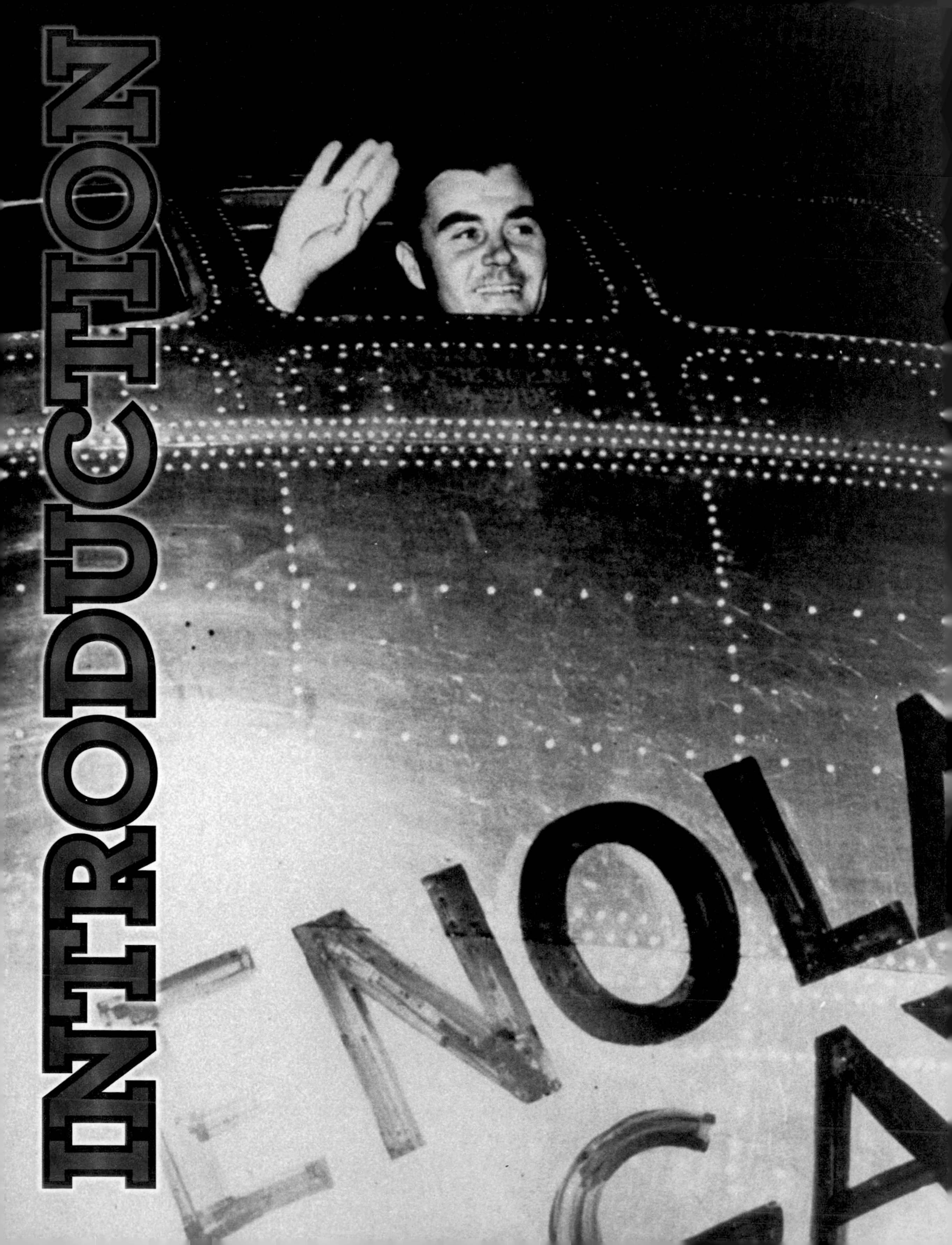

The world changed forever on Aug. 6, 1945, when a B-29 bomber called the *Enola Gay* dropped a 64-kg (140-pound) uranium-fueled atomic bomb nicknamed Little Boy on the city of Hiroshima, Japan. After the bomb exploded above the city, two-thirds of it was destroyed. A huge gust of wind and heat flattened miles of buildings and set others afire. Thousands of people burned to death. Others were hurled at high speed into buildings or killed by flying glass and debris. Of the 350,000 people present in Hiroshima that day, 140,000 were dead by the end of the year. Many of the survivors had radiation poisoning, and genetically caused birth defects due to radioactivity were common in the next generation. Never before had the world seen such a potent weapon.

The term weapons of mass destruction was coined in 1937 to refer to masses of warplanes that would bomb cities and create large-scale damage. It has since come to encompass nuclear, biological, and chemical weapons, and in this book you will learn about the scientific and political aspects of each. You will also learn how the frightening power of these weapons and their ability to destroy the entire planet has led to treaties and agreements between nations as governments have sought to limit this terrible threat to all of life.

The nuclear age began in earnest in the 1930s, as the world was hurtling toward World War II. Physicists in Europe had already described the enormous energy that would be released when an atom was split apart, and as the Nazi menace took over first Germany and then neighbouring countries, many of these scientists found their way to Britain and the United States. Fearful that Germany would create a powerful weapon based on the splitting of the atom, the U.S. government put the Europeans to work, along with many American scientists, on building such a bomb for the Allies. By 1939 physicist J. Robert Oppenheimer was already working on a way to isolate weapons-grade uranium-235, which would be the "fuel" for the bomb. In 1942 Italian-born physicist Enrico Fermi and his team at the University of Chicago produced the first self-sustaining nuclear chain reaction, a crucial step in the development of the new weapon.

In 1943 Oppenheimer was given the responsibility of running the Manhattan Project, a secret program to build a deliverable atomic bomb. He brought a team of brilliant scientists to a secret laboratory at Los Alamos, New Mexico. The Los Alamos scientists had many questionss: What fuel should they use—plutonium or uranium? How could they possibly do all the complicated calculations

Col. Paul W. Tibbets, Jr. piloted the the Enola Gay, *the B-29 bomber that dropped the atomic bomb known as Little Boy on the Japanese city of Hiroshima on Aug. 6, 1945.* National Archives/Getty Images

needed to predict a bomb's effectiveness? (Remember, this was an age before computers were ready to do the job.) What was the best way to ignite the radioactive fuel? Finally, by 1945, two designs were ready to be tried—one using uranium, the other plutonium, but both releasing a huge amount of energy after the atoms in the fuel had been made to split under massive pressure.

The bomb dropped on Hiroshima contained uranium. A few days later, a plutonium bomb nicknamed Fat Man was dropped on the city of Nagasaki, Japan. These shocking weapons were immediately followed by the end of World War II, as Japan officially surrendered on Sept. 2, 1945.

It might seem that the end of a world war would mean the end of work on nuclear weapons. But after the war, the United States and the Soviet Union quickly jockeyed for power. Soon the two former allies had divided up large chunks of the world into different spheres of influence—the Soviet Union controlled much of Eastern Europe and part of Germany, while it allied with North Korea and China. Meanwhile, the United States remained with its wartime allies in Western Europe and formed new alliances in many other parts of the world. The Cold War (1945–91) had begun. The Soviet Union was determined not to stay behind the United States in military power. The United States, meanwhile, was determined to be the leader in nuclear knowledge.

The world's first peacetime atomic weapons test was conducted on July 1, 1946, at Bikini Island in the South Pacific, in what became (along with nearby Enewatak Atoll) the Pacific Proving Grounds of the United States. Further tests would be conducted there for the next twelve years.

In 1951 the Hungarian-born physicist Edward Teller and the Polish-born mathematician Stanislaw Ulam came up with a proposal for a new, deadlier kind of nuclear weapon. They proposed that the explosive potential of a bomb would increase if it used a fuel that exploded by nuclear fusion, or the forced fusing together of atoms, instead of nuclear fission, or the splitting of atoms. Their proposal suggested a new design where the radiation generated by an atomic explosion would compress a separate chamber that held hydrogen isotopes, which would then fuse and explode. This two-stage design became known as the Teller-Ulam configuration, and it became the basis for the modern fusion, or hydrogen, bomb. It was tested in 1952 at Enewatak, creating an explosion equal to 10 million tons of TNT—500 times the strength of the bomb that flattened Nagasaki.

In 1949 Soviets tested their first atomic bomb. It was so similar to Fat Man, which exploded over Nagasaki, that it was clear that spies inside America had been giving nuclear secrets to the Soviet Union. But soon Soviets made their own scientific advances, and on Aug. 12, 1953, the Soviets tested their first hydrogen bomb, which was built from a home-grown design proposed by Russian physicist Andrey Sakharov.

Other countries also got into the act and began testing their own nuclear weapons. Great Britain followed up its wartime cooperation with the United States by developing atomic and hydrogen bombs in the 1950s. France, China, and Israel, each country determined for its own reasons to build an independent nuclear stockpile, followed suit beginning in the 1960s. India and Pakistan, once part of a single British colony, had been bitterly divided along religious lines since independence in 1947; first India and then Pakistan began to develop nuclear weapons beginning in the 1970s. Shortly after the turn of the 21st century, North Korea tested a nuclear device, and Iran embarked on what many outsiders insisted was a campaign to build nuclear weapons. Other countries that have had nuclear weapons programs but have abandoned them are South Africa, Taiwan, Argentina, Brazil, Libya, and Iraq.

Starting in the late 1950s, the Soviets began testing a new vehicle for delivering nuclear weapons called the intercontinental ballistic missile (ICBM). With ICBMs, nuclear weapons did not have to be dropped from airplanes; instead, they could be placed on self-contained missiles that had their own guidance systems. These changes made nuclear weapons more portable and easier to hide, which created even more danger. The United States soon began making its own ICBMs, too, thus intensifying the threat of nuclear war.

Other kinds of weapons of mass destruction, such as biological and chemical weapons, have also posed a threat to humankind. Five main kinds of biological agents can be weaponized and used against people, animals, or even crops. They are bacteria (such as anthrax and plague), rickettsiae (including plague), viruses (including encephalitis), fungi (including potato blight), and toxins (such as snake venom). Biological weapons have been used since ancient times, when soldiers would catapult plague victims over the walls of besieged cities, infecting people within the city walls. In most wars, diseases of various types have contributed significantly to the total death toll, whether accidentally or on purpose. In the 20th century, Germans infected Allies' horses and cows during World War I with the animal disease called glanders. During World War II, Japan did extensive testing of biological agents on prisoners of war and civilian victims, as well as Allied forces in China.

In recent years, the most frequent users of biological weapons have not been countries but terrorist groups. For example, between 1990 and 1995, a radical sect in Japan called AUM Shinrikyo attempted a series of biological attacks, using botulinum toxin and anthrax, on different targets, including a U.S. naval base on Japanese soil. However, they were unsuccessful.

Chemical weapons have proved a deadly threat since World War I. On April 22, 1915, German forces unleashed canisters of chlorine gas that floated in huge clouds across the battle lines in Ypres, Belg., choking to death some 5,000 French and Algerian troops. This weapon was made more effective because the war was mostly fought in tightly packed trenches, so soldiers could not easily run from the poison gas. Soon the Allies used chlorine and other choking gases like phosgene as well.

Blister agents such as mustard gas that can burn the skin, eyes, and lungs were also widely used in World War I. Other chemical weapons include blood agents, which keep the victim's blood from absorbing air, causing asphyxiation. Even more deadly are nerve agents such as sarin, developed by the Germans in World War II—just a single drop on the skin can paralyze and quickly kill its victims. Even after the war, the British developed the most deadly nerve agent, VX, and in 1961, at the height of the Cold War, the United States started building up large supplies of it.

Chemical weapons were also used during the 1980–88 war between Iraq and Iran. In one notorious case, the Iraqi military gassed an entire village of Kurdish people in northern Iraq. These weapons remain a potent threat as a force of terrorism.

Still, despite the dangers posed by biological and chemical weapons, the most virulent threat remains nuclear weapons. At their peaks, both the Americans and the Russians had more than 32,000 nuclear weapons. More than 500 atmospheric and more than 1,500 underground nuclear tests were conducted worldwide. By 1992 the United States alone had conducted 1,030 tests of various kinds of weapons. (After 1992, computers and nonnuclear tests were used to test America's nuclear stockpile.)

As numbers of nuclear weapons and the ease of transporting them continued to increase, politicians, academics, and military strategists became increasingly alarmed at the threat they posed to the whole world. Ironically, among the most prominent campaigners against the testing and proliferation of nuclear weapons were two of the world's greatest nuclear scientists—Oppenheimer of the United States and Sakharov of the Soviet Union. Over time, both men began to have grave doubts about the weapons they had formerly championed and developed.

Starting in the 1960s, the United States, the Soviet Union, and other countries began to cooperate on nuclear issues, beginning a series of talks that led to treaties. For example, increasing concern about the radioactive fallout in the atmosphere from multiple nuclear tests led the United States, the Soviet Union, and the United Kingdom to sign the Nuclear Test Ban Treaty on Aug. 5, 1963. It banned all tests of nuclear weapons in the atmosphere, underwater, or in outer space. Within a few months, 100 other states signed the treaty as well. In 1977 negotiations began that would end underground testing as well, but it was not until the 1990s that such testing truly ended (with the exception of

North Korea, which tested a nuclear device in 2006).

The Nuclear Non-Proliferation Treaty of 1968 allows countries that have nuclear arms to keep them, but attempts to prevent countries that do not have them from getting them. However, it also allows countries that have nuclear weapons to help other countries develop nuclear power for peacetime use. This treaty has hit certain challenges as countries such as India, Pakistan, North Korea, and possibly Iran have worked on using nuclear technology to develop nuclear weapons.

The Treaty on the Limitation of Anti-Ballistic Missile Systems (ABMs) was signed and ratified in 1972. This treaty limited the number of defensive missile systems that could be deployed by the United States and the Soviet Union to intercept each other's ICBMs. Further limitations on ICBMs and other platforms for delivering nuclear weapons were set under the Strategic Arms Limitations Talks (SALT) in 1972. In the late 1980s, U.S. Pres. Ronald Reagan and Soviet Gen. Sec. Mikhail Gorbachev signed the first Strategic Arms Reduction Talks (START) treaty, which called for the dismantling of many weapons and required inspections. Although implementation was complicated by the end of the Soviet Union, further talks have continued to require even more dismantling. The most recent START treaty was signed in 2010.

There are also treaties that ban the use of biological and chemical weapons.

By the early 21st century, more than 176 countries had ratified the Biological Weapons Convention (BWC). This treaty banned using, producing, acquiring, or stockpiling biological weapons or toxins. However, this bill allows for little oversight.

The Chemical Weapons Convention (CWC) bans the use of stockpiling, making, transferring or using chemical weapons in war. By 2007 only a few countries, including Syria and North Korea, had not signed it. While attempts had been made to limit chemical weapons since 1899, this goal was made more urgent by the more than 91,000 deaths caused by chemical weapons during World War I. The ultimate goal is a total ban, though the treaty allows some exceptions. For example, tear gas can be used for riot control within a society, but it cannot be used in war.

Readers of this volume will come to understand how treaties such as these have attempted to reduce the danger of nuclear, biological, and chemical warfare. But they will also understand that the fragile peace can be destroyed at any moment in our increasingly fragmented world. Once the brilliance of the human mind has been unleashed to create life-threatening weapons, and once these weapons—and the knowledge of how to make them—have been brought into being, it is more important than ever that responsible countries cooperate in keeping the world as safe as possible from their deadly power.

CHAPTER 1

NUCLEAR WEAPONS: THEIR PRINCIPLES AND EFFECTS

Nuclear weapons are perhaps the weapon type most commonly associated with the term *weapons of mass destruction* (WMD). A nuclear weapon is a device designed to release energy in an explosive manner as a result of nuclear fission, nuclear fusion, or a combination of the two processes. Fission weapons are commonly referred to as atomic bombs. Fusion weapons are referred to as thermonuclear bombs or, more commonly, hydrogen bombs; they are usually defined as nuclear weapons in which at least a portion of the energy is released by nuclear fusion.

Nuclear weapons produce enormous explosive energy. Their significance may best be appreciated by the coining of the words *kiloton* (1,000 tons) and *megaton* (1,000,000 tons) to describe their blast energy in equivalent weights of the conventional chemical explosive TNT. For example, the atomic bomb dropped on Hiroshima, Japan, in 1945, containing only about 64 kg (140 pounds) of highly enriched uranium, released energy equaling about 15 kilotons of chemical explosive. That blast immediately produced a strong shock wave, enormous amounts of heat, and lethal ionizing radiation. Convection currents created by the explosion drew dust and other debris into the air, creating the mushroom-shaped cloud that has since become the virtual signature of a nuclear explosion. In addition, radioactive debris was carried by winds high into the atmosphere, later to settle to Earth

Total destruction of Hiroshima, Japan, following the dropping of the first atomic bomb on Aug. 6, 1945. U.S. Air Force photo

as radioactive fallout. The enormous toll in destruction, death, injury, and sickness produced by the explosions at Hiroshima and, three days later, at Nagasaki was on a scale never before produced by any single weapon. In the decades since 1945, even as many countries have developed nuclear weapons of far greater strength than those used against the Japanese cities, concerns about the dreadful effects of such weapons have driven governments to negotiate arms control agreements such as the Nuclear Test-Ban Treaty

of 1963 and the Treaty on the Non-proliferation of Nuclear Weapons of 1968. Among military strategists and planners, the very presence of these weapons of unparalleled destructive power has created a distinct discipline, with its own internal logic and set of doctrines, known as nuclear strategy.

The first nuclear weapons were bombs delivered by aircraft. Later, warheads were developed for strategic ballistic missiles, which have become by far the most important nuclear weapons. Smaller tactical nuclear weapons have also been developed, including ones for artillery projectiles, land mines, antisubmarine depth charges, torpedoes, and shorter-range ballistic and cruise missiles.

By far the greatest force driving the development of nuclear weapons after World War II (though not by any means the only force) was the Cold War confrontation that pitted the United States and its allies against the Soviet Union and its satellite states. During this period, which lasted roughly from 1945 to 1991, the American stockpile of nuclear weapons reached its peak in 1966, with more than 32,000 warheads of 30 different types. During the 1990s, following the dissolution of the Soviet Union and the end of the Cold War, many types of tactical and strategic weapons were retired and dismantled to comply with arms control negotiations, such as the Strategic Arms Reduction Talks, or as unilateral initiatives. By 2010, the United States had approximately 9,400 warheads of nine types, including two types of bombs, three types for intercontinental ballistic missiles (ICBMs), two types for submarine-launched ballistic missiles (SLBMs), and two types for cruise missiles. Some types existed in several modifications. Of these 9,400 warheads, an estimated 2,468 were operational (that is, mated to a delivery system such as a missile); the rest were either spares held in reserve or retired warheads scheduled to be dismantled. Of the 2,468 operational warheads, approximately 1,968 were deployed on strategic (long-range) delivery systems, and some 500 were deployed on nonstrategic (short-range) systems. Of the 500 nonstrategic warheads in the U.S. arsenal, about 200 were deployed in Europe.

The Soviet nuclear stockpile reached its peak of about 33,000 operational warheads in 1988, with an additional 10,000 previously deployed warheads that had been retired but had not been taken apart. After the disintegration of the Soviet Union, Russia accelerated its warhead dismantlement program, but the status of many of the 12,000 warheads estimated to remain in its stockpile in 2010 was unclear. Given limited Russian resources and lack of legitimate military missions, only about 4,600 of these 12,000 warheads were serviceable and maintained enough to be deployed. Of the 4,600 operational warheads, some 2,600 were deployed on strategic systems and some 2,000 on nonstrategic systems. A global security concern is the safety of Russia's intact warheads and the security of nuclear materials removed from dismantled warheads.

Beginning in the 1990s, the arsenals of the United Kingdom, France, and China also underwent significant change and consolidation. Britain eliminated its land-based army, tactical naval, and air nuclear missions, so its arsenal, which contained some 350 warheads in the 1970s, had just 225 warheads in 2010. Of these, fewer than 160 were operational, all on its ballistic missile submarine fleet.

Meanwhile, France reduced its arsenal from some 540 operational warheads at the end of the Cold War to about 300 in 2010, eliminating several types of nuclear weapon systems. The Chinese stockpile remained fairly steady during the 1990s and then started to grow at the beginning of the 21st century. By 2010 China had about 240 warheads in its stockpile, some 180 of them operational and the rest in reserve or retirement. Israel maintained an undeclared nuclear stockpile of 60 to 80 warheads, but any developments were kept highly secret. India was estimated to have 60 to 80 assembled warheads and Pakistan 70 to 90. Most of India's and Pakistan's warheads were thought not to be operational, though both countries, rivals in the incipient arms race on the Indian subcontinent, were thought to be increasing their stockpiles. North Korea, which joined the nuclear club in 2006, may have produced enough plutonium by 2010 for as many as 8 to 12 warheads, though it was not clear that any of these was operational.

PRINCIPLES OF ATOMIC (FISSION) WEAPONS

When bombarded by neutrons, certain isotopes of uranium and plutonium (and some other heavier elements) will split into atoms of lighter elements, a process known as nuclear fission. In addition to this formation of lighter atoms, on average between 2.5 and 3 free neutrons are emitted in the fission process, along with

considerable energy. As a rule of thumb, the complete fission of 1 kg (2.2 pounds) of uranium or plutonium produces about 17.5 kilotons of TNT-equivalent explosive energy.

THE FISSION PROCESS

In an atomic bomb or nuclear reactor, first a small number of neutrons are given enough energy to collide with some fissionable nuclei, which in turn produce additional free neutrons. A portion of these neutrons are captured by nuclei that do not fission; others escape the material without being captured; and the remainder cause further fissions. Many heavy atomic nuclei are capable of fissioning, but only a fraction of these are fissile—that is, fissionable not only by fast (highly energetic) neutrons but also by slow neutrons. The continuing process whereby neutrons emitted by fissioning nuclei induce fissions in other fissile or fissionable nuclei is called a fission chain reaction. If the number of fissions in one generation is equal to the number of neutrons in the preceding generation, the system is said to be critical; if the number is greater than one, it is supercritical; and if it is less than one, it is subcritical. In the case of a nuclear reactor, the number of fissionable nuclei available in each generation is carefully controlled to prevent a "runaway" chain reaction. In the case of an atomic bomb, however, a very rapid growth in the number of fissions is sought.

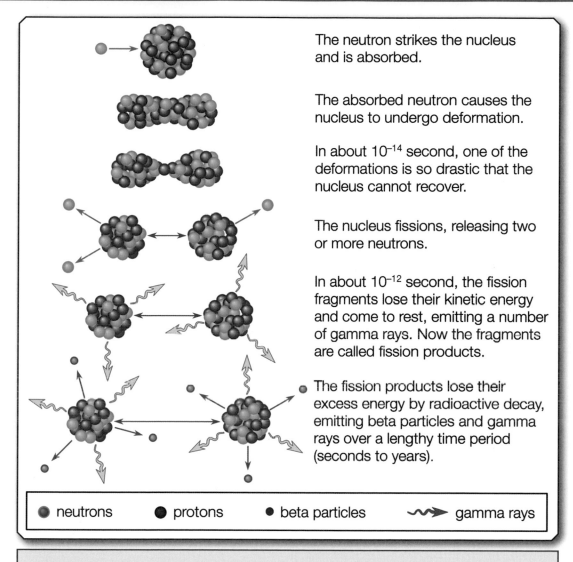

The neutron strikes the nucleus and is absorbed.

The absorbed neutron causes the nucleus to undergo deformation.

In about 10^{-14} second, one of the deformations is so drastic that the nucleus cannot recover.

The nucleus fissions, releasing two or more neutrons.

In about 10^{-12} second, the fission fragments lose their kinetic energy and come to rest, emitting a number of gamma rays. Now the fragments are called fission products.

The fission products lose their excess energy by radioactive decay, emitting beta particles and gamma rays over a lengthy time period (seconds to years).

● neutrons ● protons ● beta particles 〜〜➤ gamma rays

Sequence of events in the fission of a uranium nucleus by a neutron. Encyclopædia Britannica, Inc.

Fission weapons are normally made with materials having high concentrations of the fissile isotopes uranium-235, plutonium-239, or some combination of these; however, some explosive devices using high concentrations of uranium-233 also have been constructed and tested.

The primary natural isotopes of uranium are uranium-235 (0.7 percent), which is fissile, and uranium-238 (99.3 percent), which is fissionable but not fissile. In nature, plutonium exists only in minute concentrations, so the fissile isotope plutonium-239 is made artificially in nuclear reactors from uranium-238. In order to make an explosion, fission weapons do not require uranium or plutonium that is pure in the isotopes uranium-235 and plutonium-239. Most of the uranium used in current nuclear weapons is approximately 93.5 percent enriched uranium-235. Nuclear weapons typically contain 93 percent or more plutonium-239, less than 7 percent plutonium-240, and very small quantities of other plutonium isotopes. Plutonium-240, a by-product of plutonium production, has several undesirable characteristics, including a larger critical mass (that is, the mass required to generate a chain reaction), greater radiation exposure to workers (relative to plutonium-239), and, for some weapon designs, a high rate of spontaneous fission that can cause a chain reaction to initiate prematurely, resulting in a smaller yield. Consequently, in reactors used for the production of weapons-grade plutonium-239, the period of time that the uranium-238 is left in the reactor is restricted in order to limit the buildup of plutonium-240 to about 6 percent.

CRITICAL MASS AND THE FISSILE CORE

As is indicated above, the minimum mass of fissile material necessary to sustain a chain reaction is called the critical mass.

This quantity depends on the type, density, and shape of the fissile material and the degree to which surrounding materials reflect neutrons back into the fissile core. A mass that is less than the critical amount is said to be subcritical, while a mass greater than the critical amount is referred to as supercritical.

A sphere has the largest volume-to-surface ratio of any solid. Thus, a spherical fissile core has the fewest escaping neutrons per unit of material, and this compact shape results in the smallest critical mass, all else being equal. The critical mass of a bare sphere of uranium-235 at normal density is approximately 47 kg (104 pounds); for plutonium-239, critical mass is approximately 10 kg (22 pounds). The critical mass can be lowered in several ways, the most common being a surrounding shell of some other material that reflects some of the escaping neutrons back into the fissile core. Practical reflectors can reduce the critical mass by a factor of two or three so that about 15 kg (33 pounds) of uranium-235 and about 5 to 10 kg (11 to 22 pounds) of either plutonium-239 or uranium-233 at normal density can be made critical. The critical mass can also be lowered by compressing the fissile core because at higher densities emitted neutrons are more likely to strike a fissionable nucleus before escaping.

GUN ASSEMBLY, IMPLOSION, AND BOOSTING

In order to produce a nuclear explosion, subcritical masses of fissionable

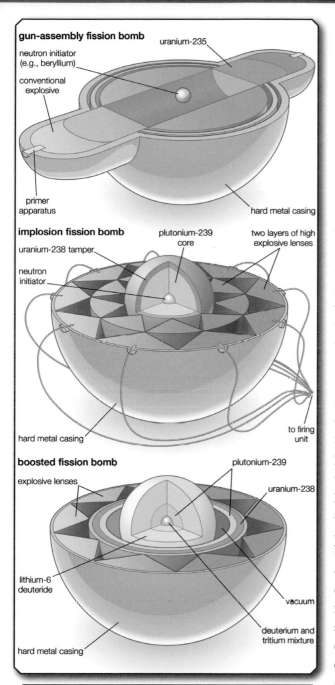

gun-assembly fission bomb

uranium-235

neutron initiator
(e.g., beryllium)

conventional
explosive

primer
apparatus

hard metal casing

implosion fission bomb

plutonium-239
core

two layers of high
explosive lenses

uranium-238 tamper

neutron
initiator

to firing
unit

hard metal casing

boosted fission bomb

plutonium-239

explosive lenses

uranium-238

lithium-6
deuteride

vacuum

deuterium and
tritium mixture

hard metal casing

*The three most common fission bomb
designs vary considerably in material and
arrangement.* © Encyclopædia Britannica, Inc.

material must be rapidly assembled into a supercritical configuration. The simplest weapon design is the pure fission gun-assembly device, in which an explosive propellant is used to fire one subcritical mass down a "gun barrel" into another subcritical mass. Plutonium cannot be used as the fissile material in a gun-assembly device because the speed of assembly in this device is too slow to preclude the high probability that a chain reaction will "pre-initiate" by spontaneous neutron emission, thereby generating an explosive yield of only a few tens of tons. Therefore, gun-assembly weapons are made with highly enriched uranium, typically more than 80 percent uranium-235.

The other major assembly method is implosion, in which a subcritical mass of fissile material is compressed by a chemical high explosive into a denser critical mass. The fissile material is typically plutonium or highly enriched uranium or a composite of the two. In the simplest design, a spherical fissile core is surrounded by a reflector (also known as a tamper), which in turn is surrounded by the chemical high explosive. Other geometries are used where the diameter of the device must be kept small—to fit, for example, in an artillery shell or missile warhead—or where higher yields are desired. To obtain a given yield, considerably less fissile material is needed for an implosion weapon than for a gun-assembly device. An implosion fission weapon with an explosive yield of one kiloton can be constructed with as little as 1 to 2 kg (2.2 to 4.4 pounds) of plutonium or with about 5 to 10 kg (11 to 22 pounds) of highly enriched uranium.

Refinements to the basic implosion design came first through Operation Sandstone, an American series of tests conducted in the spring of 1948. Three tests used implosion designs of a second generation, which incorporated composite and levitated cores. The composite core consisted of concentric shells of both uranium-235 and plutonium-239, permitting more efficient use of these fissile materials. Higher compression of the fissile material was achieved by levitating the core—that is, introducing an air gap into the weapon in order to obtain a higher yield for the same amount of fissile material.

American tests during Operation Ranger in early 1951 included implosion devices with cores containing a fraction of a critical mass—a concept originated in 1944 during the Manhattan Project. Unlike the original Fat Man design, these "fractional crit" weapons relied on compressing the fissile core to a higher density in order to achieve a supercritical mass, thereby achieving appreciable yields with less material.

Another technique for enhancing the yield of a fission explosion is called boosting. Boosting refers to a process whereby fusion reactions are used as a source of neutrons for inducing fissions at a much higher rate than could be achieved with neutrons from fission chain reactions alone. American physicist Edward Teller invented the concept by the middle of 1943. By incorporating deuterium and tritium into the core of the fissile material, a higher yield is obtained from a given quantity of fissile material—or, alternatively, the same yield is achieved with a smaller amount. The fourth American test of Operation Greenhouse, on May 24, 1951, was the first proof test of a booster design. In subsequent decades approximately 90 percent of nuclear weapons in the American stockpile relied on boosting.

PRINCIPLES OF THERMONUCLEAR (FUSION) WEAPONS

Nuclear fusion is the joining (or fusing) of the nuclei of two atoms to form a single heavier atom. At extremely high temperatures—in the range of tens of millions of degrees—the nuclei of isotopes of hydrogen (and some other light elements) can readily combine to form heavier elements and in the process release considerable energy—hence the term *hydrogen bomb*. At these temperatures, the kinetic energy of the nuclei (the energy of their motion) is sufficient to overcome the long-range electrostatic repulsive force between them, such that the nuclei can get close enough together for the shorter-range strong force to attract and fuse the nuclei—hence the term *thermonuclear*. In thermonuclear weapons, the required temperatures and density of the fusion materials are achieved with a fission explosion.

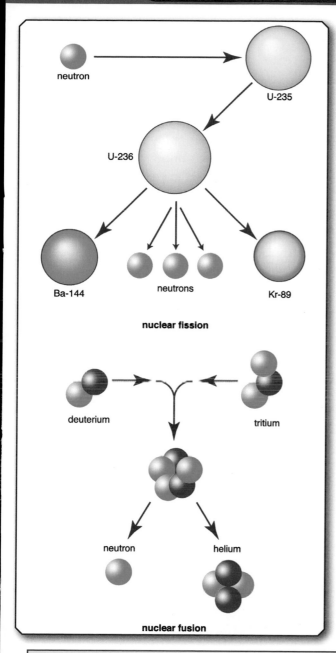

neutron

U-235

U-236

Ba-144

neutrons

Kr-89

nuclear fission

deuterium

tritium

neutron

helium

nuclear fusion

THE FUSION PROCESS

Deuterium and tritium, which are isotopes of hydrogen, provide ideal interacting nuclei for the fusion process. Two atoms of deuterium, each with one proton and one neutron, or tritium, with one proton and two neutrons, combine during the fusion process to form a heavier helium nucleus, which has two protons and either one or two neutrons. Tritium is radioactive and has a half-life of 12.32 years. The principal thermonuclear material in most thermonuclear weapons is lithium-6 deuteride, a solid chemical compound that at normal temperatures does not undergo radioactive decay. In this case, the tritium is produced in the weapon itself by neutron bombardment of the lithium-6 isotope during the course of the fusion reaction. In thermonuclear weapons, the fusion material can be incorporated directly in (or proximate to) the fissile core—for example, in the boosted fission device—or external to the fissile core, or both.

BASIC TWO-STAGE DESIGN

A typical thermonuclear warhead may be constructed according to a two-stage design, featuring a fission or

Top: Uranium-235 combines with a neutron to form an unstable intermediate, which quickly splits into barium-144 and krypton-89 plus three neutrons in the process of nuclear fission. Bottom: Deuterium and tritium combine by nuclear fusion to form helium plus a neutron. © Merriam-Webster, Inc.

boosted-fission primary (also called the trigger) and a physically separate component called the secondary. Both primary and secondary are contained within an outer metal case. Radiation from the fission explosion of the primary is contained and used to transfer energy to compress and ignite the secondary. Some of the initial radiation from the primary explosion is absorbed by the inner surface of the case, which is made of a high-density material such as uranium. Radiation absorption heats the inner surface of the case, turning it into an opaque boundary of hot electrons and ions. Subsequent radiation from the primary is largely confined between this boundary and the outer surface of the secondary capsule. Initial, reflected, and re-irradiated radiation trapped within this cavity is absorbed by lower-density material within the cavity, converting it into a hot plasma of electrons and ion particles that continue to absorb energy from the confined radiation. The total pressure in the cavity—the sum of the contribution from the very energetic particles and the generally smaller contribution from the radiation—is applied to the secondary capsule's heavy metal outer shell (called a pusher), thereby compressing the secondary.

Typically, contained within the pusher is some fusion material, such as lithium-6 deuteride, surrounding a "spark plug" of explosive fissionable material (generally uranium-235) at the centre. With the fission primary generating an explosive yield in the kiloton range, compression of the secondary is much greater than can be achieved using chemical high explosives. Compression of the spark plug results in a fission explosion that creates temperatures comparable to those of the Sun and a copious supply of neutrons for fusion of the surrounding, and now compressed, thermonuclear materials. Thus, the fission and fusion processes that take place in the secondary are generally much more efficient than those that take place in the primary.

In an efficient, modern two-stage device—such as a long-range ballistic missile warhead—the primary is boosted in order to conserve on volume and weight. Boosted primaries in modern thermonuclear weapons contain about 3 to 4 kg (6.6 to 8.8 pounds) of plutonium, while less-sophisticated designs may use double that amount or more. The secondary typically contains a composite of fusion and fissile materials carefully tailored to maximize the yield-to-weight or yield-to-volume ratio of the warhead, although it is possible to construct secondaries from purely fissile or fusion materials.

ENHANCED DESIGNS

Historically, some very high-yield thermonuclear weapons had a third, or tertiary, stage. In theory, the radiation from the tertiary can be contained and used to transfer energy to compress and ignite a fourth stage, and so on. There is no theoretical limit to the number of

Cutaway of thermonuclear warhead

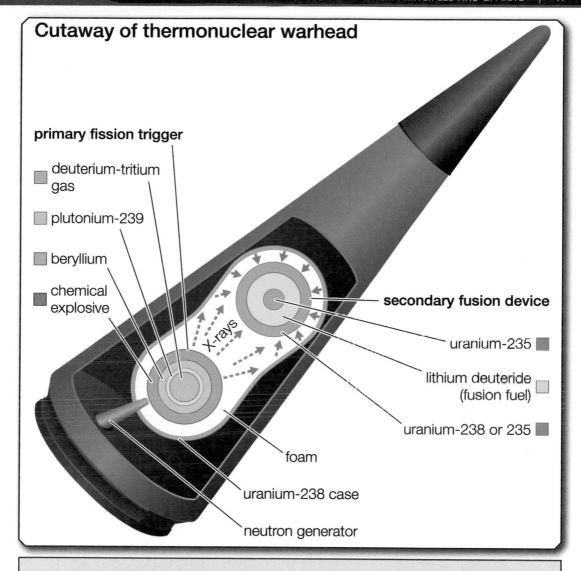

primary fission trigger

- deuterium-tritium gas
- plutonium-239
- beryllium
- chemical explosive

X-rays

secondary fusion device

- uranium-235
- lithium deuteride (fusion fuel)
- uranium-238 or 235

foam

uranium-238 case

neutron generator

The blast from a primary fission component triggers a secondary fusion explosion in a thermonuclear bomb or warhead. Encyclopædia Britannica, Inc.

stages that might be used and, consequently, no theoretical limit to the size and yield of a thermonuclear weapon. However, there is a practical limit because of size and weight limitations imposed by the requirement that the weapon be deliverable.

Uranium-238 and thorium-232 (and some other fissionable materials) cannot maintain a self-sustaining fission explosion, but these isotopes can be made to fission by an externally maintained supply of fast neutrons from fission or fusion reactions. Thus, the yield of a nuclear weapon can be increased by surrounding the device with uranium-238, in the form of either natural or depleted uranium, or with thorium-232, in the form of natural thorium. This approach is particularly advantageous in a thermonuclear weapon in which uranium-238 or thorium-232 in the outer shell of the secondary capsule is used to absorb an abundance of fast neutrons from fusion reactions produced within the secondary. The explosive yields of some weapon designs have been further increased by the substitution of highly enriched uranium-235 for uranium-238 in the secondary.

In general, the energy released in the explosion of a high-yield thermonuclear weapon stems from the boosted-fission chain reaction in the primary stage and the fissioning and "burning" of thermonuclear fuel in the secondary (and any subsequent) stage, with roughly 50 to 75 percent of the total energy produced by fission and the remainder by fusion. However, to obtain tailored weapon effects or to meet certain weight or space constraints, different ratios of fission yield to fusion yield may be employed, ranging from nearly pure fission weapons to a weapon where a very high proportion of the yield is from fusion.

Another tailored weapon is the enhanced radiation warhead, or neutron bomb, a low-yield (on the order of one kiloton), two-stage thermonuclear device designed to intensify the production of lethal fast neutrons in order to maximize mortality rates while producing less damage to buildings. The enhanced radiation is in the form of fast neutrons produced by the fusion of deuterium and tritium. The secondary contains little or no fissionable material, since this would increase the blast effect without significantly increasing the intensity of fast neutrons. The United States produced enhanced-radiation warheads for anti-ballistic missiles, short-range ballistic missiles, and artillery shells.

THE EFFECTS OF NUCLEAR WEAPONS

Nuclear weapons are fundamentally different from conventional weapons because of the vast amounts of explosive energy they can release and the kinds of effects they produce, such as high temperatures and radiation. The prompt effects of a nuclear explosion and fallout are well known through data gathered from the attacks during World War II on Hiroshima and Nagasaki, Japan; from more than 500 atmospheric and more than 1,500 underground nuclear tests conducted worldwide; and from extensive calculations and computer modeling. Longer-term effects on human health and the environment are less certain but have been extensively studied. The impacts of a nuclear explosion depend on many factors, including the design of the weapon (fission or fusion) and its yield; whether the detonation takes place in the air (and at what altitude), on the surface, underground, or underwater; the meteorological and environmental conditions; and whether the target is urban, rural, or military.

When a nuclear weapon detonates, a fireball occurs with temperatures similar to those at the centre of the Sun. The energy emitted takes several forms. Approximately 85 percent of the explosive energy produces air blast (and shock) and thermal radiation (heat). The remaining 15 percent is released as initial radiation, produced within the first minute or so, and residual (or delayed) radiation, emitted over a period of time, some of which can be in the form of local fallout.

BLAST

The expansion of intensely hot gases at extremely high pressures in a nuclear fireball generates a shock wave that expands outward at high velocity. The "overpressure," or crushing pressure, at the front of the shock wave can be measured in pascals (or kilopascals; kPa) or in pounds per square inch (psi). The greater the overpressure, the more likely that a given structure will be damaged by the sudden impact of the wave front. A related destructive effect comes from the "dynamic pressure," or high-velocity wind, that accompanies the shock wave. An ordinary two-story, wood-frame house will collapse at an overpressure of 34.5 kPa (5 psi). A one-megaton weapon exploded at an altitude of 3,000 metres (10,000 feet) will generate overpressure

of this magnitude out to 7 km (about 4 miles) from the point of detonation. The winds that follow will hurl a standing person against a wall with several times the force of gravity. Within 8 km (5 miles) few people in the open or in ordinary buildings will likely be able to survive such a blast. Enormous amounts of masonry, glass, wood, metal, and other debris created by the initial shock wave will fly at velocities above 160 km (100 miles) per hour, causing further destruction.

THERMAL RADIATION

As a rule of thumb, approximately 35 percent of the total energy yield of an airburst is emitted as thermal radiation—light and heat capable of causing skin burns and eye injuries and starting fires of combustible material at considerable distances. The shock wave, arriving later, may spread fires further. If the individual fires are extensive enough, they can coalesce into a mass fire known as a firestorm, generating a single convective column of rising hot gases that sucks in fresh air from the periphery. The inward-rushing winds and the extremely high temperatures generated in a firestorm consume virtually everything combustible. At Hiroshima the incendiary effects were quite different from those at Nagasaki, in part because of differences in terrain. The firestorm that raged over the level terrain of Hiroshima left 11.4 square km (4.4 square miles) severely damaged—roughly four times the area burned in the hilly terrain of Nagasaki.

Initial Radiation

A special feature of a nuclear explosion is the emission of nuclear radiation, which may be separated into initial radiation and residual radiation. Initial radiation, also known as prompt radiation, consists of gamma rays and neutrons produced

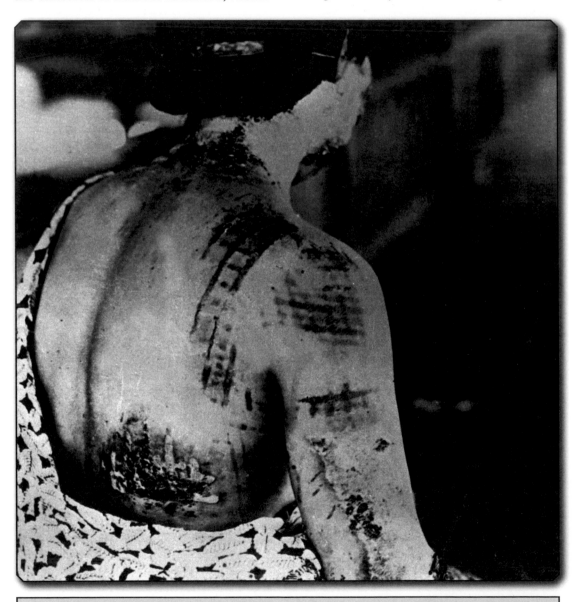

Photograph of a woman's skin burned in the pattern of the kimono she was wearing at the time of her exposure to radiation from one of the atomic bombs dropped by the United States on Japan. National Archives and Records Administration/Department of Defense

within a minute of the detonation. Beta particles (free electrons) and a small proportion of alpha particles (helium nuclei, i.e., two protons and two neutrons bound together) are also produced, but these particles have short ranges and typically will not reach Earth's surface if the weapon is detonated high enough above ground. Gamma rays and neutrons can produce harmful effects in living organisms, a hazard that persists over considerable distances because of their ability to penetrate most structures. Though their energy is only about 3 percent of the total released in a nuclear explosion, they can cause a considerable proportion of the casualties.

RESIDUAL RADIATION AND FALLOUT

Residual radiation is defined as radiation emitted more than one minute after the detonation. If the fission explosion is an airburst, the residual radiation will come mainly from the weapon debris. If the explosion is on or near the surface, the soil, water, and other materials in the vicinity will be sucked upward by the rising cloud, causing early (local) and delayed (worldwide) fallout. Early fallout settles to the ground during the first 24 hours; it may contaminate large areas and be an immediate and extreme biological hazard. Delayed fallout, which arrives after the first day, consists of microscopic particles that are dispersed by prevailing winds and settle in low concentrations over possibly extensive portions of Earth's surface.

A nuclear explosion produces a complex mix of more than 300 different isotopes of dozens of elements, with half-lifes from fractions of a second to millions of years. The total radioactivity of the fission products is extremely large at first, but it falls off at a fairly rapid rate as a result of radioactive decay.

NUCLEAR WINTER

Nuclear winter was a type of environmental devastation that certain scientists during the Cold War contended would probably result from the hundreds of nuclear explosions likely to take place during a nuclear war. The damaging effects of the light, heat, blast, and radiation caused by nuclear explosions had long been known to scientists, but the indirect effects of such explosions on the environment remained largely ignored for decades. In the 1970s, however, several studies posited that the layer of ozone in the stratosphere that shields living things from much of the Sun's harmful ultraviolet radiation might be depleted by the large amounts of nitrogen oxides produced by nuclear explosions. Further studies speculated that large amounts of dust kicked up into the atmosphere by nuclear explosions might block sunlight from reaching Earth's surface, leading to a temporary cooling of the air. Scientists then began to take into account the smoke produced by vast forests set ablaze by nuclear fireballs, and in 1983 an ambitious study, known as the TTAPS study (from the initials of the last names of its authors,

R.P. Turco, O.B. Toon, T.P. Ackerman, J.B. Pollack, and Carl Sagan), took into consideration the crucial factor of smoke and soot arising from the burning petroleum fuels and plastics in nuclear-devastated cities. (Smoke from such materials absorbs sunlight much more effectively than smoke from burning wood.) The TTAPS study coined the term nuclear winter, *and its ominous hypotheses about the environmental effects of a nuclear war came under intensive study by both the American and Soviet scientific communities.*

The basic cause of nuclear winter, as hypothesized by researchers, would be the numerous and immense fireballs caused by exploding nuclear warheads. These fireballs would ignite huge uncontrolled fires (firestorms) over any and all cities and forests that were within range of them. Great plumes of smoke, soot, and dust would be sent aloft from these fires, lifted by their own heating to high altitudes where they could drift for weeks before dropping back or being washed out of the atmosphere onto the ground. Several hundred million tons of this smoke and soot would be shepherded by strong west-to-east winds until they would form a uniform belt of particles encircling the Northern Hemisphere from 30° to 60° latitude. These thick black clouds could block out all but a fraction of the Sun's light for a period as long as several weeks. Surface temperatures would plunge for a few weeks as a consequence, perhaps by as much as 11 to 22 °C (20 to 40 °F). The conditions of semidarkness, killing frosts, and subfreezing temperatures, combined with high doses of radiation from nuclear fallout, would interrupt plant photosynthesis and could thus destroy much of Earth's vegetation and animal life. The extreme cold, high radiation levels, and the widespread destruction of industrial, medical, and transportation infrastructures along with food supplies and crops would trigger a massive death toll from starvation, exposure, and disease. A nuclear war could thus reduce Earth's human population to a fraction of its previous numbers.

A number of scientists immediately disputed the results of the original calculations. Though a nuclear war on the scale once feared between the United States and the Soviet Union would undoubtedly be devastating, the degree of damage to life on Earth ceased being a matter of controversy once the Cold War antagonisms ended.

Seven hours after a nuclear explosion, residual radioactivity will have decreased to about 10 percent of its amount at 1 hour, and after another 48 hours it will have decreased to 1 percent. (The rule of thumb is that for every sevenfold increase in time after the explosion, the radiation dose rate decreases by a factor of 10.)

ELECTROMAGNETIC PULSE

A nuclear electromagnetic pulse (EMP) is the time-varying electromagnetic radiation resulting from a nuclear explosion. The development of the EMP is shaped by the initial nuclear radiation from the explosion—specifically, the gamma radiation. High-energy electrons are produced

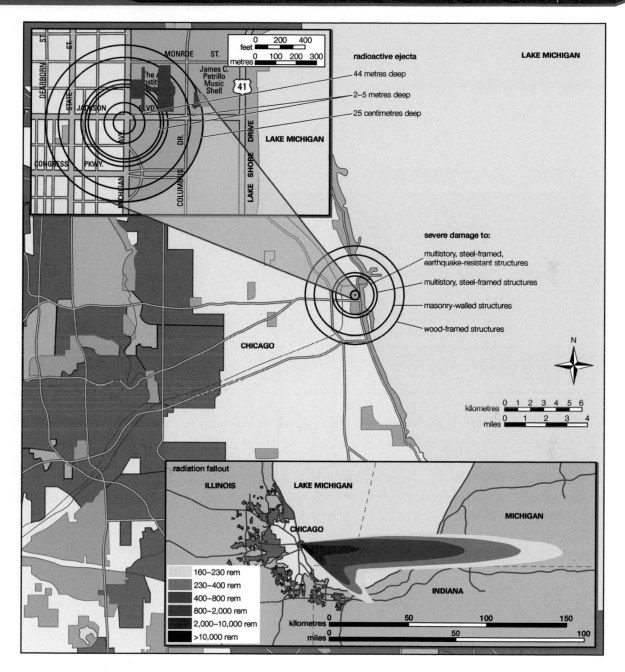

Blast and radiation effects at different ranges for a 500-kiloton nuclear explosion detonated at ground level. Encyclopædia Britannica, Inc.

in the environment of the explosion when gamma rays collide with air molecules (a process called the Compton effect). Positive and negative charges in the atmosphere are separated as the lighter, negatively charged electrons are swept away from the explosion point and the heavier, positively charged ionized air molecules are left behind. This charge separation produces a large electric field. Asymmetries in the electric field are caused by factors such as the variation in air density with altitude and the proximity of the explosion to Earth's surface. These asymmetries result in time-varying electrical currents that produce the EMP. The characteristics of the EMP depend strongly on the height of the explosion above the surface.

EMP was first noticed in the United States in the 1950s when electronic equipment failed because of induced currents and voltages during some nuclear tests. In 1960 the potential vulnerability of American military equipment and weapons systems to EMP was officially recognized. EMP can damage unprotected electronic equipment, such as radios, radars, televisions, telephones, computers, and other communication equipment and systems. EMP damage can occur at distances of tens, hundreds, or thousands of kilometres from a nuclear explosion, depending on the weapon yield and the altitude of the detonation. For example, in 1962 a failure of electronic components in street lights in Hawaii and activation of numerous automobile burglar alarms in Honolulu were attributed to a high-altitude U.S. nuclear test at Johnston Atoll, some 1,300 km (800 miles) to the southwest. For a high-yield explosion of approximately 10 megatons detonated 320 km (200 miles) above the centre of the continental United States, almost the entire country, as well as parts of Mexico and Canada, would be affected by EMP. Procedures to improve the ability of networks, especially military command and control systems, to withstand EMP are known as "hardening."

CHAPTER 2

THE UNITED STATES: THE FIRST NUCLEAR POWER

The principles of nuclear fission—and the terrific energy that would be released by such a reaction—were elucidated by European scientists during the 1930s. That decade also saw the rise of totalitarian regimes on the European continent and the looming threat of war around the world, and as a consequence many atomic physicists made their way to the United Kingdom and the United States. The latter country, already the "arsenal of democracy" in the great death-struggle against totalitarianism, yoked its engineering might to scientific theory and became the first country to build (and the only country ever to use) atomic weapons.

After World War II the new Cold War against the Soviet Union spurred the United States to explore the development of even more powerful weapons based on nuclear fusion. In the early 1950s it became the first country to test and deploy hydrogen bombs.

THE FIRST ATOMIC BOMBS

The United States produced the first atomic bombs—under the pressures of World War II. Reacting to the possibility that the Allies' wartime enemies might beat them in a race to such weapons, and also wishing to put a stop to the most destructive war the world had ever seen, the United States put together a crash program to build weapons of unprecedented power.

DISCOVERY OF NUCLEAR FISSION

Following the discovery of the neutron by the British physicist James Chadwick in 1932 and artificial radioactivity by the French chemists Frédéric and Irène Joliot-Curie in 1934, the Italian physicist Enrico Fermi performed a series of experiments in which he exposed many elements to low-speed neutrons. When he exposed thorium and uranium, chemically different radioactive products resulted, indicating that new elements had been formed rather than merely different isotopes of the original elements. Many scientists concluded that Fermi had produced elements beyond uranium, the last element in the periodic table at the time, and so these elements became known as transuranium elements. In 1938 Fermi received the Nobel Prize for Physics for his work.

Meanwhile, in Germany, Otto Hahn and Fritz Strassmann discovered that a radioactive barium isotope resulted from bombarding uranium with neutrons. The low-speed neutrons caused the uranium nucleus to fission, or break apart into two smaller pieces; the combined atomic numbers of the two pieces—for example, barium and krypton—equaled that of the uranium nucleus. To be sure of this surprising result, Hahn sent his findings to his colleague Lise Meitner, an Austrian Jew who had fled to Sweden. With her nephew Otto Frisch, Meitner concurred in the results and recognized the enormous energy potential.

In early January 1939, Frisch rushed to Copenhagen to inform the Danish scientist Niels Bohr of the discovery. Bohr was about to leave for a visit to the United States, where he reported the news to colleagues. The revelation set off experiments at many laboratories, and nearly 100 articles were published about the exciting phenomenon by the end of the year. Bohr, working with John Wheeler at Princeton University in Princeton, N.J., postulated that the uranium isotope uranium-235 was the one undergoing fission; the other isotope, uranium-238, merely absorbed the neutrons. It was discovered that neutrons were also produced during the fission process; on average, each fissioning atom produced more than two neutrons. If the proper amount of material were assembled, these free neutrons might create a chain reaction. Under special conditions, a very fast chain reaction might produce a very large release of energy—in short, a weapon of fantastic power might be feasible.

PRODUCING A CONTROLLED CHAIN REACTION

The possibility that an atomic bomb might first be developed by Nazi Germany alarmed many scientists and was drawn to the attention of U.S. Pres. Franklin D. Roosevelt by German-born physicist Albert Einstein, then living in the United States. The president appointed an Advisory Committee on Uranium, which reported on Nov. 1, 1939, that a chain reaction in uranium was possible, though unproved. Chain-reaction experiments with carbon and uranium were started in New York City at Columbia University, and in March 1940 it was confirmed that the isotope uranium-235 was responsible for low-speed neutron fission in uranium. The Advisory Committee on Uranium increased its support of the Columbia experiments and arranged for a study of possible methods for separating the uranium-235 isotope from the much more abundant uranium-238. (Naturally occurring uranium contains approximately 0.7 percent uranium-235, with most of the remainder being uranium-238.) The centrifuge process, in which the heavier isotope is spun to the outside, at first seemed the most useful method of isolating uranium-235. However, a rival process was proposed at Columbia in which gaseous uranium hexafluoride is diffused through barriers, or filters; slightly more molecules containing the lighter isotope, uranium-235, would pass through the filter than those containing the heavier isotope, slightly enriching the mixture on the far side. Using the gaseous diffusion method, more than a thousand stages, occupying many acres, were needed to enrich the mixture to 90 percent uranium-235.

During the summer of 1940, Edwin McMillan and Philip Abelson of the University of California at Berkeley discovered element 93 (naming it neptunium, after the next planet after Uranus, for which uranium was named); they inferred that this element would decay into element 94. The Bohr and Wheeler fission theory suggested that one of the isotopes of this new element might also fission under low-speed neutron bombardment. Glenn T. Seaborg and his group, also at the University of California at Berkeley, discovered element 94 on Feb. 23, 1941, and during the following year they named it plutonium, made enough for experiments, and established its fission characteristics. Low-speed neutrons did indeed cause it to undergo fission and at a rate much higher than that of uranium-235. The Berkeley group, under physicist Ernest Lawrence, was also considering producing large quantities of uranium-235 by turning one of their cyclotrons into a super mass spectrograph. A mass spectrograph employs a magnetic field to bend a current of uranium ions; the heavier ions (such as uranium-238) bend at a larger radius than the lighter ions (such as uranium-235), allowing the two separated currents to be collected in different receivers.

In May 1941 a review committee reported that a nuclear explosive probably could not be available before 1945. A chain reaction in natural uranium was probably 18 months off, and it would take at least an additional year to produce enough plutonium and three to five years to separate enough uranium-235 for a bomb. Further, it was held that all of these estimates were optimistic. In late June 1941 President Roosevelt established the Office of Scientific Research and Development under the direction of the scientist Vannevar Bush, subsuming the National Defense Research Committee that had directed the nation's mobilization effort to utilize science for weapon development the previous year.

In the fall of 1941 the Columbia chain-reaction experiment with natural uranium and carbon yielded negative results. A review committee concluded that boron impurities might be poisoning it by absorbing neutrons. It was decided to transfer all such work to the University of Chicago and repeat the experiment there with high-purity carbon. This eventually led to the world's first controlled nuclear chain reaction, achieved by Fermi and his group on Dec. 2, 1942, in the squash court under the stands of the university's Stagg Field. At Berkeley, the cyclotron, converted into a mass spectrograph (later called a calutron), was exceeding expectations in separating uranium-235, and it was enlarged to a 10-calutron system capable of producing almost 3 grams (about 0.1 ounce) of uranium-235 per day.

FOUNDING THE MANHATTAN PROJECT

The United States' entry into World War II in December 1941 was decisive in providing funds for a massive research and production effort for obtaining fissionable materials, and in May 1942 the momentous decision was made to proceed simultaneously on all promising production methods. Vannevar Bush decided that the army should be brought into the production plant construction activities. The U.S. Army Corps of Engineers was given the job in mid-June, and Col. James C. Marshall was selected to head the project. Soon an office in New York City was opened, and in August the project was officially given the name Manhattan Engineer District— hence Manhattan Project, the name by which this effort would be known ever afterward. Over the summer, Bush and others felt that progress was not proceeding quickly enough, and the army was pressured to find another officer that would take more decisive action. Col. Leslie R. Groves replaced Marshall on September 17 and immediately began making major decisions from his headquarters office in Washington, D.C. After his first week, a workable oversight arrangement was achieved with the formation of a three-man military policy committee chaired by Bush (with chemist James B. Conant as his alternate) along with representatives from the army and the navy.

Throughout the next few months, Groves (by then a brigadier general) chose the three key sites—Oak Ridge, Tenn.; Los Alamos, N.M.; and Hanford, Wash.— and selected the large corporations to build and operate the atomic factories. In December contracts were signed with the DuPont Company to design, construct, and operate the plutonium production reactors and to develop the plutonium separation facilities. Two types of factories to enrich uranium were built at Oak Ridge.

On November 16 Groves and physicist J. Robert Oppenheimer visited the Los Alamos Ranch School, some 100 km (60 miles) north of Albuquerque, N.M., and on November 25 Groves approved it as the site for the main scientific laboratory, often referred to by its code name Project Y.

ROBERT OPPENHEIMER

Julius Robert Oppenheimer was born on April 22, 1904, in New York City, the son of a German immigrant who had made his fortune by importing textiles. During his undergraduate studies at Harvard University, Oppenheimer excelled in Latin, Greek, physics, and chemistry, published poetry, and studied Oriental philosophy. After graduating in 1925, he sailed for England to do research at the Cavendish Laboratory at the University of Cambridge, which, under the leadership of Lord Ernest Rutherford, had an international reputation for its pioneering studies on atomic structure. Max Born invited Oppenheimer to Göttingen University, where, in 1927, he received his doctorate. After short visits at science centres in Leiden and Zürich, he returned to the United States to teach physics at the University of California at Berkeley and the California Institute of Technology.

Oppenheimer's early research was devoted in particular to energy processes of subatomic particles, including electrons, positrons, and cosmic rays. Since quantum theory had been proposed only a few years before, the university post provided him an excellent opportunity to devote his entire career to the exploration and development of its full significance. In addition, he trained a whole generation of U.S. physicists, who were greatly affected by his qualities of leadership and intellectual independence.

The rise of Adolf Hitler in Germany stirred his first interest in politics. In 1936 he sided with the republic during the Civil War in Spain, where he became acquainted with Communist students. Although his father's death in 1937 left Oppenheimer a fortune that allowed him to subsidize anti-Fascist organizations, the tragic suffering inflicted by Joseph Stalin on Russian scientists led him to withdraw his associations with the Communist Party—in fact, he never joined the party—and at the same time reinforced in him a liberal democratic philosophy.

After the invasion of Poland by Nazi Germany in 1939, Oppenheimer then began to seek a process for the separation of uranium-235 from natural uranium and to determine the critical mass of uranium required to make such a bomb. In August 1942 the U.S. Army was given the responsibility of organizing the efforts of British

J. Robert Oppenheimer. Alfred Eisenstaedt/Time & Life Pictures/ Getty Images

and U.S. physicists to seek a way to harness nuclear energy for military purposes, an effort that became known as the Manhattan Project. Oppenheimer was instructed to establish and administer a laboratory to carry out this assignment. In 1943 he persuaded Gen. Leslie Groves, head of the Manhattan Project, to choose the plateau of Los Alamos, near Santa Fe, N.M., as the site for the laboratory.

For reasons that have not been made clear, Oppenheimer in 1942 initiated discussions with military security agents that culminated with the implication that some of his friends and acquaintances were agents of the Soviet government. This led to the dismissal of a personal friend on the faculty at the University of California. In a 1954 security hearing he described his contribution to those discussions as "a tissue of lies."

The joint effort of outstanding scientists at Los Alamos culminated in the first nuclear explosion on July 16, 1945, at the Trinity Site near Alamogordo, N.M., after the surrender of Germany. In October of the same year, Oppenheimer resigned his post. In 1947 he became head of the Institute for Advanced Study (IAS) in Princeton, N.J., and served from 1947 until 1952 as chairman of the General Advisory Committee of the Atomic Energy Commission, which in October 1949 opposed development of the hydrogen bomb.

On Dec. 21, 1953, Oppenheimer was notified of a military security report unfavourable to him and was accused of having associated with Communists in the past, of delaying the naming of Soviet agents, and of opposing the building of the hydrogen bomb. A security hearing declared him not guilty of treason but ruled that he should not have access to military secrets. As a result, his contract as adviser to the Atomic Energy Commission was cancelled. The Federation of American Scientists immediately came to his defense with a protest against the trial. Oppenheimer was made the worldwide symbol of the scientist, who, while trying to resolve the moral problems that arise from scientific discovery, becomes the victim of a witch-hunt. He spent the last years of his life working out ideas on the relationship between science and society.

In 1963 Pres. Lyndon B. Johnson presented Oppenheimer with the Enrico Fermi Award of the Atomic Energy Commission. Oppenheimer retired from the IAS in 1966 and died of throat cancer the following year, on Feb. 18, 1967, in Princeton.

The previous month, Groves had decided to choose Oppenheimer to be the scientific director of the laboratory where the design, development, and final manufacture of the weapon would take place. By July 1943 two essential and encouraging pieces of experimental data had been obtained—plutonium did give off neutrons in fission, more than uranium-235; and the neutrons were emitted in a short time compared to that needed to bring the weapon materials into a supercritical assembly. The theorists working on the project contributed one discouraging note, however, as their estimate of the critical mass for uranium-235 had risen more than threefold, to something between 23 and 45 kg (50 and 100 pounds).

SELECTING A WEAPON DESIGN

The emphasis during the summer and fall of 1943 was on the gun method of assembly, in which the projectile, a subcritical piece of uranium-235 (or plutonium-239), would be placed in a gun barrel and fired into the target, another subcritical piece. After the mass was joined (and now supercritical), a neutron source would be used to start the chain reaction. A problem developed with applying the gun method to plutonium, however. In manufacturing plutonium-239 from uranium-238 in a reactor, some of the plutonium-239 absorbed a neutron and became plutonium-240. This material underwent spontaneous fission, producing neutrons. Some neutrons would always be present in a plutonium assembly and would cause it to begin multiplying as soon as it "went critical" but before it reached supercriticality; the assembly would then explode prematurely and produce comparatively little energy. The gun designers tried to overcome this problem by achieving higher projectile speeds, but they lost out in the end to a better idea—the implosion method.

In late April 1943 a Project Y physicist, Seth H. Neddermeyer, proposed the first serious theoretical analysis of implosion. His arguments showed that it would be feasible to compress a solid sphere of plutonium by surrounding it with high explosives and that this method would be superior to the gun method both in its higher velocity and in its shorter path of assembly. John von Neumann, a mathematician who had experience in working on shaped-charge, armour-piercing projectiles, supported the implosion method enthusiastically and went on to be a major contributor to the design of the high-explosive "lenses" that would focus the compression inward. Physicist Edward Teller suggested that because the material was compressed, less of it would be needed. By late 1943 the implosion method was being given a higher priority, and by July 1944 it had become clear that an efficient gun-assembly device could not be built with plutonium. Los Alamos' central research mission rapidly shifted to solve the new challenge. Refinements in design eventually resulted in a solid 6-kg (13-pound) sphere of plutonium, with a small hole in the centre for the neutron initiator, that would be compressed by imploding lenses of high explosive.

RACING TO BUILD THE BOMBS

By 1944 the Manhattan Project was spending money at a rate of more than $1 billion per year. The situation was likened to a horse race—no one could say which of the horses (the calutron plant, the diffusion plant, or the plutonium reactors) was likely to win or whether any of them would even finish the race. In July 1944 the first Y-12 calutrons had been running for three months but were operating at less than 50 percent efficiency; the main problem was in recovering the large amounts of material that splattered throughout the innards of the calutron without reaching the uranium-235 or uranium-238 receiver bins. The gaseous diffusion plant, known as K-25, was far from completion, with the production of satisfactory barriers remaining the major problem. And the first plutonium reactor at Hanford had been turned on in September, but it had promptly turned itself off. Solving this problem, which proved to be caused by absorption of neutrons by one of the fission products, took several months. These delays meant almost certainly that the war in Europe would be over before the weapon could be ready. The ultimate target was slowly changing from Germany to Japan.

Within 24 hours of Roosevelt's death on April 12, 1945, Pres. Harry S. Truman was told briefly about the atomic bomb by Secretary of War Henry L. Stimson. On April 25 Stimson, with Groves's assistance, gave Truman a more extensive briefing on the status of the project: the uranium-235 gun design had been finalized, but a sufficient quantity of uranium-235 would not be accumulated until about August 1. Enough plutonium-239 would be available for an implosion assembly to be tested in early July; a second would be ready in August. Several dozen B-29

bombers had been modified to carry the weapons, and construction of a staging base was under way at Tinian, in the Mariana Islands, 2,400 km (1,500 miles) south of Japan.

The test of the plutonium weapon was named Trinity; it was fired at 5:29:45 AM on July 16, 1945, at the Alamogordo Bombing Range in south-central New Mexico. The theorists' predictions of the energy release, or yield, of the device ranged from the equivalent of less than 1,000 tons of TNT to the equivalent of 45,000 tons (that is, from 1 to 45 kilotons of TNT). The test actually produced a yield of about 21,000 tons.

THE WEAPONS ARE USED

A single B-29 bomber named *Enola Gay* flew over Hiroshima, Japan, on Monday, Aug. 6, 1945, at 8:15 AM. The untested uranium-235 gun-assembly bomb, nicknamed Little Boy, was airburst 580 metres (1,900 feet) above the city to maximize destruction; it was later estimated to yield 15 kilotons. Two-thirds of the city area was destroyed. The population present at the time was estimated at 350,000; of these, 140,000 died by the end of the year. The second weapon, a duplicate of the plutonium-239 implosion assembly tested in Trinity and nicknamed Fat Man, was to be dropped on Kokura on August 11; a third was being prepared in the United States for possible use 7 to 10 days later. To avoid bad weather, the schedule for Fat Man was moved

On Aug. 8, 1945, two days after detonating a uranium-fueled atomic bomb over Hiroshima, Japan, the United States dropped a plutonium-fueled atomic bomb over the Japanese port of Nagasaki. U.S. Department of Defense

up two days to August 9. A B-29 named *Bockscar* spent 45 minutes over Kokura without sighting its aim point. The air crew then proceeded to the secondary target of Nagasaki, where at 11:02 AM the weapon was airburst at 500 metres (1,650 feet); it was later estimated that the explosion yielded 21 kilotons. About half of Nagasaki was destroyed, and about 70,000 of some 270,000 people present at the time of the blast died by the end of the year.

THE FIRST HYDROGEN BOMBS

Having demonstrated the awful power of the atomic bomb, which it credited with ending World War II, the United States found itself as the leader of a new Cold War against the communist powers, led by the Soviet Union, which was soon well on its way to building its own atomic bombs. The arms race continued with the United States' development in the decade after World War II of thermonuclear weapons.

ORIGINS OF THE "SUPER"

U.S. research on thermonuclear weapons was started by a conversation in September 1941 between Fermi and Teller. Fermi wondered if the explosion of a fission weapon could ignite a mass of deuterium sufficiently to begin nuclear fusion. (Deuterium, an isotope of hydrogen with one proton and one neutron in the nucleus—i.e., twice the normal weight—makes up 0.015 percent of natural hydrogen and can be separated in quantity by electrolysis and distillation. It exists in liquid form only below about -250 °C, or -418 °F, depending on pressure.) Teller undertook to analyze thermonuclear processes in some detail and presented his findings to a group of theoretical physicists convened by Oppenheimer in Berkeley in the summer of 1942. One participant, Emil Konopinski, suggested that the use of tritium be investigated as a thermonuclear fuel, an insight that would later be important to most designs. (Tritium, an isotope of hydrogen with one proton and two neutrons in the nucleus—i.e., three times the normal weight—does not exist in nature except in trace amounts, but it can be made by irradiating lithium in a nuclear reactor.)

As a result of these discussions, the participants concluded that a weapon based on thermonuclear fusion was possible. When the Los Alamos laboratory was being planned, a small research program on the Super, as the thermonuclear design came to be known, was included. Several conferences were held at the laboratory in late April 1943 to acquaint the new staff members with the existing state of knowledge and the direction of the research program. The consensus was that modest thermonuclear research should be pursued along theoretical lines. Teller proposed more intensive investigations, and some work did proceed, but the more urgent

EDWARD TELLER

Edward Teller (or, in Hungarian, Ede Teller) was born on Jan. 15, 1908, in Budapest to a family of prosperous Hungarian Jews. He earned a degree in chemical engineering at the Institute of Technology in Karlsruhe, Ger., and then went to Munich and Leipzig to earn a Ph.D. in physical chemistry (1930).

During the years of the Weimar Republic, Teller was absorbed with atomic physics, first studying under Niels Bohr in Copenhagen and then teaching at the University of Göttingen (1931–33). In 1935 Teller and his bride, Augusta Harkanyi, went to the United States, where he taught at George Washington University in Washington, D.C.

By 1941 Teller had taken out U.S. citizenship and joined Enrico Fermi's team at the University of Chicago in the epochal experiment to produce the first self-sustaining nuclear chain reaction. Teller then accepted an invitation from the University of California, Berkeley, to work on theoretical studies on the atomic bomb with J. Robert Oppenheimer; and when Oppenheimer set up the secret Los Alamos Scientific Laboratory in New Mexico in 1943, Teller was among the first men recruited. Although the Los Alamos assignment was to build a fission bomb, Teller digressed more and more from the main line of research to continue his own inquiries into a potentially much more powerful thermonuclear hydrogen fusion bomb.

Teller accepted a position with the Institute for Nuclear Studies at the University of Chicago in 1946 but returned to Los Alamos as a consultant for extended periods. The Soviet Union's explosion of an atomic bomb in 1949 made him more determined that the United States have a hydrogen bomb, but the Atomic Energy Commission's General Advisory Committee, which was headed by Oppenheimer, voted against a crash program to develop one. The debate was settled by the confession of the British atomic scientist Klaus Fuchs that he had passed early American data on a hydrogen bomb to the Soviets. In response, Pres. Harry Truman ordered the go-ahead on the weapon, and Teller laboured on at Los Alamos to make it a reality.

Teller and his colleagues at Los Alamos made little actual progress in designing a workable thermonuclear device until 1951, when Teller and physicist Stanislaw Ulam came up with the proposal that the radiation generated by an atomic bomb's explosion be used to compress and ignite a thermonuclear second core. This provided a firm basis for a fusion weapon, and a device using the Teller-Ulam configuration, as it is now known, was successfully tested on Nov. 1, 1952; it yielded an explosion equivalent to 10 million tons (10 megatons) of TNT. Teller became known in the United States as "the father of the H-bomb." (Ulam's role did not emerge from classified documents and other sources until nearly three decades after the event.)

At government hearings held in 1954 to determine whether Oppenheimer was a security risk, Teller's testimony was decidedly unsympathetic to his former chief. "I would feel personally more secure," he told the inquiry board, "if public matters would rest in other hands."

Oppenheimer's security clearance was revoked, and his career as a science administrator was at an end. Although Teller's testimony was by no means the decisive factor in this outcome, many prominent American nuclear physicists never forgave him for what they viewed as his betrayal of Oppenheimer.

Teller was instrumental in the creation of the United States' second nuclear weapons laboratory, the Lawrence Livermore National Laboratory, in Livermore, Calif., in 1952, and he was its associate director or director from 1954 to 1975. Concurrently he was professor of physics at the University of California, Berkeley, from 1953 to 1960 and was professor-at-large there until 1970.

A staunch anticommunist, Teller devoted much time in the rest of his life to his crusade to keep the United States ahead of the Soviet Union in nuclear arms. He died on Sept. 9, 2003, in Stanford, Calif.

task of developing a fission weapon always took precedence—a necessary prerequisite for a thermonuclear bomb in any event.

In the fall of 1945, after the success of the atomic bomb and the end of World War II, the future of the Manhattan Project, including Los Alamos and the other facilities, was unclear. Government funding was severely reduced, many scientists returned to universities and to their careers, and contractor companies turned to other pursuits. The Atomic Energy Act, signed by President Truman on Aug. 1, 1946, established the Atomic Energy Commission (AEC), replacing the Manhattan Engineer District, and gave it civilian authority over all aspects of atomic energy, including oversight of nuclear warhead research, development, testing, and production.

From April 18 to 20, 1946, a conference led by Teller at Los Alamos reviewed the status of the Super. At that time it was believed that a fission weapon could be used to ignite one end of a cylinder of liquid deuterium and that the resulting thermonuclear reaction would self-propagate to the other end. This conceptual design was known as the "classical Super."

One of the two central design problems was how to ignite the thermonuclear fuel. It was recognized early on that a mixture of deuterium and tritium theoretically could be ignited at lower temperatures and would have a faster reaction time than deuterium alone, but the question of how to achieve ignition remained unresolved. The other problem, equally difficult, was whether and under what conditions burning might proceed in thermonuclear fuel once ignition had taken place. An exploding thermonuclear weapon involves many extremely complicated, interacting physical and nuclear processes. The speeds of the exploding materials can be up to millions of metres per second, temperatures and pressures are greater than those at the centre of the Sun, and timescales are billionths of a second. To resolve whether the classical Super or any other design would work required accurate numerical models of these processes—a formidable task, especially as the computers needed to perform the calculations were still under development. Also, the requisite fission triggers were not yet ready, and the limited resources of Los Alamos could not support an extensive program.

POLICY DIFFERENCES, TECHNICAL PROBLEMS

On Sept. 23, 1949, President Truman announced, "We have evidence that within recent weeks an atomic explosion occurred in the U.S.S.R." This first Soviet test stimulated an intense four-month secret debate about whether to proceed with the hydrogen bomb project. One of the strongest statements of opposition against proceeding with the program came from the General Advisory Committee (GAC) of the AEC, chaired by Oppenheimer. In their report of Oct. 30, 1949, the majority recommended "strongly against" initiating an all-out effort, believing "that the extreme dangers to mankind inherent in the proposal wholly outweigh any military advantages that could come from

this development." "A super bomb," they went on to say, "might become a weapon of genocide" and "should never be produced." Two members went even further, stating: "The fact that no limits exist to the destructiveness of this weapon makes its very existence and the knowledge of its construction a danger to humanity as a whole. It is necessarily an evil thing considered in any light." Nevertheless, the Joint Chiefs of Staff, State Department, Defense Department, Joint Committee on Atomic Energy, and a special subcommittee of the National Security Council all recommended proceeding with the hydrogen bomb. On Jan. 31, 1950, Truman announced that he had directed the AEC to continue its work on all forms of nuclear weapons, including hydrogen bombs.

In the months that followed Truman's decision, the prospect of building a thermonuclear weapon seemed less and less likely. Mathematician Stanislaw M. Ulam, with the assistance of Cornelius J. Everett, had undertaken calculations of the amount of tritium that would be needed for ignition of the classical Super. Their results were spectacular and discouraging: the amount needed was estimated to be enormous. In the summer of 1950, more detailed and thorough calculations by other members of the Los Alamos Theoretical Division confirmed Ulam's estimates. This meant that the cost of the Super program would be prohibitive.

Also in the summer of 1950, Fermi and Ulam calculated that liquid deuterium probably would not "burn"—that is, there would probably be no self-sustaining and propagating reaction. Barring surprises, therefore, the theoretical work to 1950 indicated that every important assumption regarding the viability of the classical Super was wrong. If success was to come, it would have to be accomplished by other means.

THE TELLER-ULAM CONFIGURATION

The other means became apparent between February and April 1951, following breakthroughs achieved at Los Alamos. One breakthrough was the recognition that the burning of thermonuclear fuel would be more efficient if a high density were achieved throughout the fuel prior to raising its temperature, rather than the classical Super approach of just raising the temperature in one area and then relying on the propagation of thermonuclear reactions to heat the remaining fuel. A second breakthrough was the recognition that these conditions—high compression and high temperature throughout the fuel—could be achieved by containing and converting the radiation from an exploding fission weapon and then using this energy to compress a separate component containing the thermonuclear fuel.

The major figures in these breakthroughs were Ulam and Teller. In

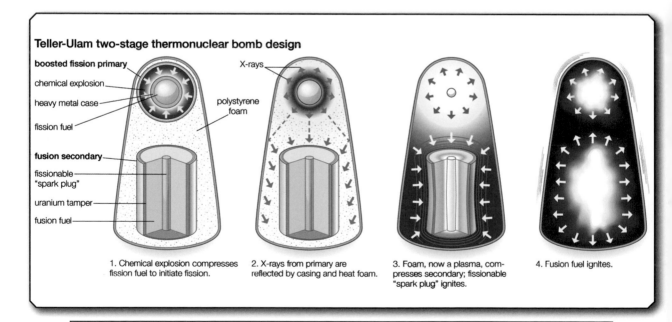

Teller-Ulam two-stage thermonuclear bomb design

- boosted fission primary
- chemical explosion
- heavy metal case
- fission fuel
- polystyrene foam
- X-rays
- fusion secondary
- fissionable "spark plug"
- uranium tamper
- fusion fuel

1. Chemical explosion compresses fission fuel to initiate fission.

2. X-rays from primary are reflected by casing and heat foam.

3. Foam, now a plasma, compresses secondary; fissionable "spark plug" ignites.

4. Fusion fuel ignites.

Teller-Ulam two-stage thermonuclear bomb design. Encyclopædia Britannica, Inc.

December 1950 Ulam had proposed a new fission weapon design, using the mechanical shock of an ordinary fission bomb to compress to a very high density a second fissile core. (This two-stage fission device was conceived entirely independently of the thermonuclear program, its aim being to use fissionable materials more economically.) Early in 1951, Ulam went to see Teller and proposed that the two-stage approach be used to compress and ignite a thermonuclear secondary. Teller suggested radiation implosion, rather than mechanical shock, as the mechanism for compressing the thermonuclear fuel in the second stage. On March 9, 1951, Teller and Ulam presented a report containing both alternatives, titled "On Heterocatalytic Detonations I: Hydrodynamic Lenses and Radiation Mirrors." A second report, dated April 4, by Teller, included some extensive calculations by Frederic de Hoffmann and elaborated on how a thermonuclear bomb could be constructed. The two-stage radiation implosion design proposed by these reports, which led to the modern concept of thermonuclear weapons, became known as the Teller-Ulam configuration.

THE WEAPONS ARE TESTED

It was immediately clear to all scientists concerned that these new ideas—achieving a high density in the thermonuclear fuel by compression using a fission primary—provided for the first time a firm basis for a fusion weapon. Without hesitation, Los Alamos adopted the new program. Gordon Dean, chairman of the AEC, convened a meeting at the Institute for Advanced Study in Princeton, N.J., hosted by Oppenheimer, on June 16–17, 1951, where the new idea was discussed. In attendance were the GAC members, AEC commissioners, and key scientists and consultants from Los Alamos and Princeton. The participants were unanimously in favour of active and rapid pursuit of the Teller-Ulam principle.

Just prior to the conference, on May 8 at Enewetak atoll in the western Pacific, a test explosion named George had successfully used a fission bomb to ignite a small quantity of deuterium and tritium. The original purpose of George had been to confirm the burning of these thermonuclear fuels (about which there had never been any doubt), but with the new conceptual understanding contributed by Teller and Ulam, the test provided the bonus of successfully demonstrating radiation implosion.

In September 1951, Los Alamos proposed a test of the Teller-Ulam concept for November 1952. Richard L. Garwin, a 23-year-old University of Chicago postgraduate student of Enrico Fermi's, who was at Los Alamos in the summer of 1951, was primarily responsible for transforming Teller and Ulam's theoretical ideas into a workable engineering design for the device used in

The first thermonuclear weapon (hydrogen bomb), code-named Mike, was detonated at Enewetak atoll in the Marshall Islands, Nov. 1, 1952. Three of a series of photographs taken at an altitude of 3,600 metres (12,000 feet) 80 km (50 miles) from the detonation site. U.S. Air Force photo.

the Mike test. The device weighed 82 tons, in part because of cryogenic (low-temperature) refrigeration equipment necessary to keep the deuterium in liquid form. It was successfully detonated during Operation Ivy, on Nov. 1, 1952, at Enewetak. The explosion achieved a yield of 10.4 megatons (million tons), 500 times larger than the Nagasaki bomb, and it produced a crater 1,900 metres (6,240 feet) in diameter and 50 metres (164 feet) deep.

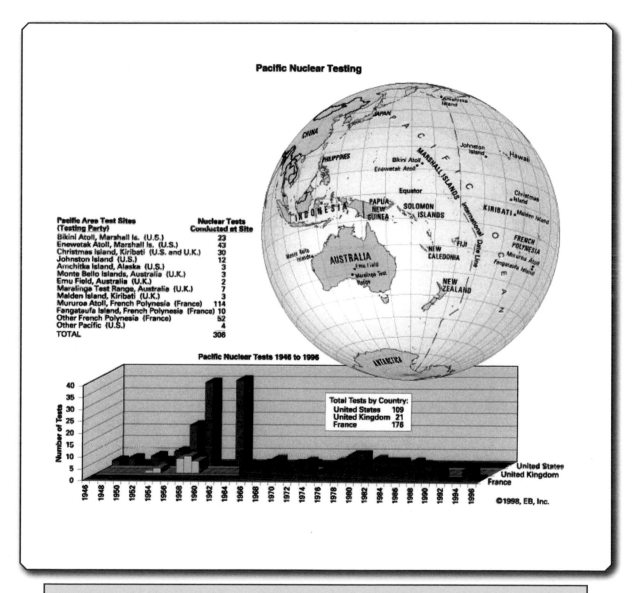

Pacific Nuclear Testing

Pacific Area Test Sites (Testing Party)	Nuclear Tests Conducted at Site
Bikini Atoll, Marshall Is. (U.S.)	23
Enewetak Atoll, Marshall Is. (U.S.)	43
Christmas Island, Kiribati (U.S. and U.K.)	30
Johnston Island (U.S.)	12
Amchitka Island, Alaska (U.S.)	3
Monte Bello Islands, Australia (U.K.)	3
Emu Field, Australia (U.K.)	2
Maralinga Test Range, Australia (U.K.)	7
Malden Island, Kiribati (U.K.)	3
Mururoa Atoll, French Polynesia (France)	114
Fangataufa Island, French Polynesia (France)	10
Other French Polynesia (France)	52
Other Pacific (U.S.)	4
TOTAL	306

Pacific Nuclear Tests 1946 to 1996

Total Tests by Country:
United States 109
United Kingdom 21
France 176

©1998, EB, Inc.

Islands in the South Pacific were used extensively for nuclear tests between 1945 and 1995.

BIKINI ATOLL

Bikini Atoll is a part of the Ralik (western) chain of the Marshall Islands in the central Pacific Ocean. Lying north of the Equator, it is 360 km (225 miles) northwest of Kwajalein and 305 km (190 miles) east of Enewetak Atoll. It consists of a ring of about 20 small coral islands whose average elevation is only some 2.1 metres (7 feet) above low tide level. The area of the group amounts to little more than 5 square km (2 square miles) of dry land, distributed about the edges of an oval lagoon 40 km (25 miles) long and 24 km (15 miles) wide. The largest islands are Bikini and Enyu (or Eneu). The atoll was known before World War II as Escholtz Atoll. It was administered by the United States from 1947 as part of the U.S. Trust Territory of the Pacific Islands under a United Nations trusteeship until it became part of the Republic of the Marshall Islands in 1979.

After Japan had been driven from the Marshall Islands in 1944, the islands and atolls, Bikini among them, came under the administration of the U.S. Navy. In 1946 Bikini became the site of Operation Crossroads, a vast military-scientific experiment to determine the impact of atomic bombs on naval vessels. The tests made it necessary to first relocate the atoll's 166 native Micronesians to Rongerik and then to Kili Island, about 800 km (500 miles) southeast of Bikini. The world's first peacetime atomic-weapons test was conducted at Bikini on July 1, 1946. A 20-kiloton atomic bomb was dropped from an airplane and exploded in the air over a fleet of about 80 obsolete World War II naval vessels, among them battleships and aircraft carriers, all of them unmanned. The second test, on July 25, was the world's first underwater atomic explosion; it raised an enormous column of radioactive water that sank nine ships. Further tests, some of them thermonuclear, were conducted from 1954 to 1958, when Bikini, together with Enewetak Atoll, constituted the Pacific Proving Ground of the United States Atomic Energy Commission. In 1956 Bikini was the test site of the first hydrogen bomb dropped by a U.S. airplane.

The atoll suffered serious radioactive contamination from these tests. In 1969 the U.S. government began work on a long-range project to reclaim the land and, ultimately, to repatriate the Bikinian population. Some native islanders began returning to Bikini in the late 1960s, but they had to be moved back to Kili in 1978 when it became clear that radioactivity levels at Bikini were still dangerously high. In 1985, in response to a lawsuit filed by Bikini islanders, the U.S. government agreed to fund a cleanup of the island chain. Work began in 1991, and the first cleanup project was completed in 1998. However, radiation levels were still considered too high to allow resettlement, although they were deemed low enough to permit tourism on the atoll. In 1996 it was opened for scuba diving among the lagoon's sunken warships, and sport fishing began two years later.

FURTHER REFINEMENTS

With the Teller-Ulam configuration proved, deliverable thermonuclear weapons were designed and initially tested during Operation Castle in 1954. The first test of the series, conducted on March 1, 1954, was called Bravo. It used solid lithium deuteride rather than liquid deuterium and produced a yield of 15 megatons, 1,000 times as large as the Hiroshima bomb. Here the principal

The goal of Operation Castle was to produce a practical, deliverable thermonuclear bomb. The United States' Mike thermonuclear device—detonated Nov. 1, 1952, at Enewetak, an atoll in the Marshall Islands—had weighed some 82 tons and took up the space of a small building to hold the cryogenic equipment that kept its deuterium fuel in liquid form. In contrast, Bravo, the first test of the Operation Castle series, used solid lithium deuteride, forgoing the need for cryogenic equipment. Detonated on March 1, 1954, at Bikini, another atoll in the Marshall Islands, the Bravo bomb produced a 15-megaton explosion—three times the expected yield. The large blast produced considerable unexpected radiation, which resulted in widespread contamination that forced the U.S. government to make restitution to various injured parties. Lawrence Livermore National Laboratory (LLNL)

thermonuclear reaction was the fusion of deuterium and tritium. The tritium was produced in the weapon itself by neutron bombardment of the lithium-6 isotope in the course of the fusion reaction. Using lithium deuteride instead of liquid deuterium eliminated the need for cumbersome cryogenic equipment.

With the completion of Castle, the feasibility of lightweight, solid-fuel thermonuclear weapons was proved. Vast quantities of tritium would not be needed after all. Refinements of the basic two-stage Teller-Ulam configuration resulted in thermonuclear weapons with a wide variety of characteristics and applications. Some high-yield deliverable weapons incorporated additional thermonuclear fuel (lithium deuteride)

and fissionable material (uranium-235 and uranium-238) in a third stage. The largest American bombs had yields of 10 to 25 megatons and weighed up to 20 tons. Beginning in the early 1960s, however, the United States built a variety of smaller, lighter weapons that exhibited steadily improving yield-to-weight and yield-to-volume ratios. By the time nuclear testing ended in 1992, the United States had conducted 1,030 tests of weapons of every conceivable shape, size, and purpose. After 1992, computers and nonnuclear tests were used to validate the safety and reliability of America's nuclear stockpile—though the view was widely held that entirely new computer-generated weapon designs could not be considered reliable without actual testing.

CHAPTER 3

THE OTHER NUCLEAR POWERS

During World War II, scientists in several countries performed experiments in connection with nuclear reactors and fission weapons. By the time the war began on Sept. 1, 1939, Germany had a special office for the military application of nuclear fission, where chain-reaction experiments with uranium and graphite were being planned and ways of separating the uranium isotopes were under study. Some measurements on graphite, later shown to be in error, led physicist Werner Heisenberg to recommend that heavy water be used, instead, for the moderator. This dependence on scarce heavy water was a major reason the German experiments never reached a successful conclusion. The isotope separation studies were oriented toward low enrichments (about 1 percent uranium-235) for the chain reaction experiments; they never got past the laboratory apparatus stage, and several times these prototypes were destroyed in bombing attacks. As for the fission weapon itself, it was a rather distant goal, and practically nothing but "back-of-the-envelope" studies were done on it.

Like their counterparts elsewhere, Japanese scientists initiated research on an atomic bomb. In December 1940, Japan's leading nuclear scientist, Nishina Yoshio, undertook a small-scale research effort supported by the armed forces. It did not progress beyond the laboratory because of a lack of government support, resources, and uranium.

In the decades after the war, however, first the United Kingdom and the Soviet Union, then France and China, joined their old World War II ally, the United States, in a growing "club" of nuclear-armed countries that squared off against one another in the great ideological confrontation of the Cold War. Elsewhere in the world, other countries, seeking advantage or prestige in their own regional rivalries, took advantage of the almost inevitable spread of nuclear technology and expertise to build their own nuclear arsenals. By the end of the 20th century the threat of nuclear weapons was less to be found in an all-out war between the old Cold War superpowers than it was in the proliferation of nuclear weapons to lesser powers responding to a multitude of political and military antagonisms.

THE UNITED KINGDOM

British scientists were deeply involved in the U.S. Manhattan Project during World War II, and this experience was used after the war to begin the United Kingdom's own nuclear weapons program.

ATOMIC WEAPONS

The British atomic weapon project started informally, as in the United States, among university physicists. In April 1940 a short paper by Otto Frisch and Rudolf Peierls, expanding on the idea of critical mass, estimated that a superweapon could be built using several pounds of pure uranium-235 and that this amount of material might be obtainable from a chain of diffusion tubes. This three-page memorandum was the first report to foretell with scientific conviction the practical possibility of making a bomb

and the horrors it would bring. A group of scientists known as the MAUD committee was set up in the Ministry of Aircraft Production in April 1940 to decide if a uranium bomb could be made. The committee approved a report on July 15, 1941, concluding that the scheme for a uranium bomb was practicable, that work should continue on the highest priority, and that collaboration with the Americans should be continued and expanded. As the war took its toll on the economy, the British position evolved through 1942 and 1943 to one of full support for the American project with the realization that Britain's major effort would come after the war. While the British program was sharply reduced at home, approximately 90 scientists and engineers went to the United States at the end of 1943 and during 1944 to work on various aspects of the Manhattan Project. The valuable knowledge and experience they acquired sped the development of the British atomic bomb after 1945.

After the war a formal decision to manufacture a British atomic bomb was made by Prime Minister Clement Attlee's government during a meeting of the Defence Subcommittee of the Cabinet in early January 1947. The construction of a first reactor to produce fissile material and associated facilities had got under way the year before. William Penney, a member of the British team at Los Alamos, N.M., U.S., during the war, was placed in charge of fabricating and testing the bomb, which was to be of a plutonium type similar to the one dropped on Nagasaki, Japan. That Britain was developing nuclear

Three RAF Canberra bombers fly over Cyprus in 1955. By 1954, many Canberra bombers were armed with atomic bombs. © AP Images

weapons was not made public until Feb. 17, 1952, when Prime Minister Winston Churchill declared plans to test the first British-made atomic bomb at the Monte Bello Islands, off the northwest coast of Australia; Churchill made the official announcement in a speech before the House of Commons on February 26, at which time he also reported that the country had the manufacturing infrastructure to ensure regular production of the bomb. On Oct. 3, 1952, the first British atomic weapons test, called Hurricane, was successfully conducted aboard the frigate HMS *Plym*, with an estimated yield of 25 kilotons. By early 1954, Royal Air Force (RAF) Canberra bombers were armed with atomic bombs. Under a program known as Project E, squadrons of Canberras as well as Valiant bombers were supplied with American nuclear bombs—until early 1965 for Bomber Command in the United Kingdom and until 1969 for the Royal Air Force in Germany—before being replaced with British models.

THERMONUCLEAR WEAPONS

The formal decision to develop thermonuclear weapons was made in secret on June 16, 1954, by a small Defence Policy Committee chaired by Churchill. The prime minister informed the cabinet on July 7, arguing that Britain needed the most modern weapons if it was to remain a world power. A discussion ensued that day and the next to consider questions of cost, morality, world influence and standing, proliferation, and public opinion. Cabinet agreement was reached later that month to support plans to produce hydrogen bombs. More than six months would pass before the public learned of the decision. Minister of Defence Harold Macmillan announced in his Statement on Defence on Feb. 17, 1955, that the United Kingdom planned to develop and produce hydrogen bombs. A debate in the House of Commons took place the first two days of March, and Churchill gave a riveting speech on why Britain must have these new weapons.

At that point British scientists did not know how to make a thermonuclear bomb, a situation similar to their American counterparts after President Truman's directive of January 1950. An important first step was to put William Cook in charge of the program. Cook, chief of the Royal Naval Scientific Service and a mathematician, was transferred to Aldermaston, a government research and development laboratory and manufacturing site in Berkshire, where he arrived in September to be deputy director to William Penney. Over the next year the staff increased and greater resources were committed to solving the difficult scientific and engineering problems they faced. The goal was to produce a one-megaton weapon. *Megaton* was defined loosely, and boosted designs (with yields in the hundreds of kilotons) were proposed to meet it. To achieve a modern Teller-Ulam design, a consensus began to form around a staged device with compression of the secondary. These ideas were informed by analyzing the debris from the 1954 Castle series of tests by the United States as well as Joe-19, the Soviet Union's successful test in November 1955 of its first true two-stage thermonuclear bomb. Precisely how the essential ideas emerged and evolved and when the design was finalized remain unclear, but by the spring of 1956 there was growing confidence that solutions were close at hand. The British thermonuclear project, like its American and Soviet counterparts, was a team effort in which the work of many people led to eventual success. Among major contributors were Keith Roberts, Bryan Taylor, John Corner, and Ken Allen.

Sites in the middle of the Pacific Ocean at Christmas Island and at Malden Island were chosen to test several designs of prototype weapons in the spring of 1957. Three devices were tested in May and June at Malden, the second one a huge fission bomb, slightly boosted, producing a yield of 720 kilotons. Though the first and third tests did demonstrate staging and radiation implosion, their yields of 300 and 200 kilotons were disappointing, indicating that there were still design problems. On the morning of November 8, a two-stage device inside a Blue Danube case was successfully detonated at 2,200 metres (7,200 feet) over Christmas Island, with a yield calculated at 1.8 megatons. Britain now had an effective thermonuclear bomb. Further refinements in design to make lighter, more compact, and more efficient bombs culminated in a three-megaton test on April 28, 1958, and four more tests in August and September. Conducted just before a nuclear test moratorium that began in October 1958 and lasted until September 1961, this final series of British atmospheric tests solidified the boosted designs and contributed novel ideas to modern thermonuclear weapons.

THE BRITISH DETERRENT FORCE

From 1962 to 1991 Britain conducted 24 underground tests jointly with the United States at the U.S. test site in Nevada to develop warheads for several types of aircraft bombs and missile warheads. During the 1950s the RAF's "V-bomber" force of Valiant, Vulcan, and Victor aircraft was introduced into service to carry a variety of fission and fusion bombs. In June 1969 the strategic deterrent role was transferred to the Royal Navy's Polaris submarine force, and in the 1990s these boats were replaced by Vanguard-class submarines carrying American Trident II ballistic missiles armed with British warheads. RAF aircraft continued to serve in other roles until March 1998, when the last British nuclear bombs were withdrawn from service.

THE SOVIET UNION

At the end of World War II, the Soviet Union drew upon its own considerable scientific expertise as well as information gleaned from U.S. weapons programs to enter the club of nuclear powers. Its nuclear arsenal grew to become the world's largest during the Cold War arms race.

ATOMIC WEAPONS

In the decade before World War II, Soviet physicists were actively engaged in nuclear and atomic research. By 1939 they had established that, once uranium has been fissioned, each nucleus emits neutrons and can therefore, at least in theory, begin a chain reaction. The following year, physicists concluded that such a chain reaction could be ignited in either natural uranium or its isotope uranium-235 and that this reaction could be sustained and controlled with a moderator such as heavy water. In July 1940 the Soviet Academy of Sciences established the Uranium Commission to study the "uranium problem."

By February 1939 news had reached Soviet physicists of the discovery of nuclear fission in the West. The military implications of such a discovery were immediately apparent, but Soviet research was brought to a halt by the

German invasion in June 1941. In early 1942 Soviet physicist Georgy N. Flerov noticed that articles on nuclear fission were no longer appearing in Western journals—an indication that research on the subject had become classified. In response, Flerov wrote to, among others, Premier Joseph Stalin, insisting that "we must build the uranium bomb without delay." In 1943 Stalin ordered the commencement of a research project under the supervision of Igor V. Kurchatov, who had been director of the nuclear physics laboratory at the Physico-Technical Institute of the Academy of Sciences in Leningrad. Under Kurchatov's direction, Laboratory No. 2 was established in April to conduct the new program. (After the war it was renamed the Laboratory of Measurement Devices of the Academy of Sciences and subsequently became the Russian Research Centre Kurchatov Institute.) Kurchatov initiated work on three fronts: designing an experimental uranium pile and achieving a chain reaction, exploring methods to separate the isotope uranium-235, and—after receiving Western intelligence about its feasibility as a weapon material—studying the properties of plutonium and how it might be produced.

Throughout 1944 the scale of the program remained small. The war ground on, the prospects of an actual weapon seemed remote, and scarce funds kept the number of employees working under Kurchatov limited. By the time of the Potsdam Conference, which brought the Allied leaders together the day after

the Trinity test was conducted by the United States in July 1945, the project on the atomic bomb was about to change dramatically. During one session at the conference, Truman remarked to Stalin that the United States had built a "new weapon of unusual destructive force." Stalin replied that he would like to see the United States make "good use of it against the Japanese."

After the Americans dropped two bombs on Japan in early August 1945, the full force of the importance of this new weapon finally hit Stalin, and he ordered a crash program to have an atomic bomb as quickly as possible. In late August a Special Committee chaired by Lavrenty P. Beria, chief of the NKVD (Soviet secret police and forerunner of the KGB), was established to oversee the Soviet version of the Manhattan Project. Over the next four years the full resources of the Soviet Union were mobilized to build the bomb, including extensive use of prison labour from the Gulag to mine uranium and build the plants. The first Soviet chain reaction took place in Moscow on Dec. 25, 1946, using an experimental graphite-moderated natural uranium pile known as F-1. The first plutonium production reactor became operational at the Chelyabinsk-40 (later known as Chelyabinsk-65 and now Ozersk) complex in the Ural Mountains, on June 19, 1948. Eight months later the first batch of plutonium was produced. After separating the irradiated uranium fuel in the nearby radio-chemical plant, it was converted into plutonium metal and shaped into hemispheres. The components then went to the "Installation" (KB-11), located in what became the secret Soviet city of Sarov, 400 km (250 miles) southeast of Moscow, for final assembly. Later known as Arzamas-16 (currently the All-Russian Scientific Research Institute of Experimental Physics), the secret laboratory was similar to Los Alamos in that the first bombs were designed and assembled there.

The role of espionage in the making of the Soviet atomic bomb has been acknowledged since 1950, with the arrests in Britain of the German-born Klaus Fuchs and in the United States of the American couple Julius and Ethel Rosenberg. New information made available from Russian sources following the breakup of the Soviet Union in 1991, however, demonstrated that espionage was more extensive than previously known and was more important to the Soviets' success. Throughout the war and afterward, Beria's spies amassed significant amounts of technical data that saved Kurchatov and his team valuable time and scarce resources. The first Soviet test occurred on Aug. 29, 1949, using a plutonium device (known in the West as Joe-1) with a yield of approximately 20 kilotons. A direct copy of the Fat Man bomb tested at Trinity and dropped on Nagasaki, Joe-1 was based on plans supplied by Fuchs and by Theodore A. Hall, the latter a second key spy at Los Alamos whose activities were discovered only after the dissolution of the Soviet Union.

JULIUS AND ETHEL ROSENBERG

Ethel Greenglass was born on May 12, 1918, in New York City. After her graduation from high school in 1931, she worked as a clerk for some years and then married Julius Rosenberg (born Sept. 28, 1915, also in New York) in 1939, the year Julius earned a degree in electrical engineering. By then, the two were already active members of the Communist Party. In the following year Julius obtained a job as a civilian engineer with the U.S. Army Signal Corps, and he and Ethel began working together to disclose U.S. military secrets to the Soviet Union. Later, Ethel's brother, Sgt. David Greenglass, who was assigned as a machinist to the Manhattan Project to build the atomic bomb, provided the Rosenbergs with data on nuclear weapons. The Rosenbergs turned over this information to Harry Gold, a Swiss-born courier for the espionage ring, who then passed it to Anatoly A. Yakovlev, the Soviet Union's vice-consul in New York City.

Julius Rosenberg was discharged by the army in 1945 for having lied about his membership in the Communist Party. Gold was arrested on May 23, 1950, in connection with the case of the British spy Klaus Fuchs, who had been arrested for giving U.S. and British nuclear secrets to the Soviet Union. The arrests of Greenglass and Julius Rosenberg followed quickly in June and

July, and Ethel was arrested in August. Another conspirator, Morton Sobell, a college class-mate of Julius Rosenberg, fled to Mexico but was extradited.

The Rosenbergs were charged with espionage and brought to trial on March 6, 1951; David Greenglass was the chief witness for the prosecution. On March 29 they were found guilty, and on April 5 the couple was sentenced to death. (Sobell and Gold received 30-year prison terms, and Greenglass, who was tried separately, was sentenced to 15 years in prison.) For two years the Rosenberg case was appealed through the courts and before world opinion. The constitutionality and applicability of the Espionage Act of 1917, under which the Rosenbergs were tried, as well as the impartiality of the trial judge, Irving R. Kaufman—who in pronouncing sentence had accused them of a crime "worse than murder"—were key issues during the appeals process. Seven different appeals reached the Supreme Court of the United States and were denied, and pleas for executive clemency were dismissed by Pres. Harry Truman in 1952 and Pres. Dwight Eisenhower in 1953. A worldwide campaign for mercy failed, and the Rosenbergs were executed in the electric chair at Sing Sing Prison in Ossining, N.Y., on June 19, 1953. Ethel became the first woman executed in the United States since Mary Surratt was hanged in 1865 for her alleged role in the assassination of Abraham Lincoln.

In the years after the Rosenbergs' executions, there was significant debate about their guilt. The two were frequently regarded as victims of cynical and vindictive officials of the FBI. Highly sympathetic portraits of the Rosenbergs were offered in major novels, including E.L. Doctorow's The Book of Daniel *(1971) and Robert Coover's* The Public Burning *(1977). (The former was released as the motion picture* Daniel *in 1983.) The controversy over their guilt was largely resolved in the early 1990s after the fall of communism in the Soviet Union and the release of Soviet intelligence information that confirmed the Rosenbergs' involvement in espionage.*

THERMONUCLEAR WEAPONS

In June 1948 Igor Y. Tamm was appointed to head a special research group at the P.N. Lebedev Physics Institute (FIAN) to investigate the possibility of building a thermonuclear bomb. Andrey Sakharov joined Tamm's group and, with his colleagues Vitaly Ginzburg and Yury Romanov, worked on calculations produced by Yakov Zeldovich's group at the Institute of Chemical Physics.

As recounted by Sakharov, the Russian discovery of the major ideas behind the thermonuclear bomb went through several stages.

The first design, proposed by Sakharov in 1948, consisted of alternating layers of deuterium and uranium-238 between a fissile core and a surrounding chemical high explosive. Known as Sloika ("Layer Cake"), the design was refined by Ginzburg in 1949 through the substitution of lithium-6 deuteride for the liquid deuterium. When bombarded with neutrons, lithium-6 breeds tritium, which can fuse with deuterium to release more energy.

In March 1950 Sakharov arrived at KB-11. Under the scientific leadership of Yuly Khariton, work at KB-11 had begun three years earlier to develop and produce Soviet nuclear weapons. Members of the Tamm and the Zeldovich groups also went to KB-11 to work on the thermonuclear bomb. A Layer Cake bomb, known in the West as Joe-4 and in the Soviet Union as RDS-6, was detonated on Aug. 12, 1953, with a yield of 400 kilotons. Significantly, it was a deliverable thermonuclear bomb—a milestone that the United States would not reach until May 20, 1956—and also the first use of solid lithium-6 deuteride. Finally, a more efficient two-stage nuclear configuration using radiation compression (analogous to the Teller-Ulam design) was detonated on Nov. 22, 1955. Known in the West as Joe-19 and RDS-37 in the Soviet Union, the thermonuclear bomb was dropped from a bomber at the Semipalatinsk (now Semey, Kazakh.) test site. As recounted by Sakharov, this test "crowned years of effort [and] opened the way for a whole range of devices with remarkable capabilities... it had essentially solved the problem of creating high-performance thermonuclear weapons."

The Soviet Union conducted 715 tests between 1949 and 1990, out of which came a wide variety of weapons, from nuclear artillery shells to multimegaton missile warheads and bombs. On Oct. 30, 1961, the Soviet Union detonated a 58-megaton nuclear device, later revealed to have been tested at approximately half of its optimal design yield.

ANDREY SAKHAROV

Andrey Dmitriyevich Sakharov was born on May 21, 1921, in Moscow. His exceptional scientific promise was recognized early, and in 1938 he enrolled in the physics department of Moscow State University. After the outbreak of war with Germany in June 1941, he and his fellow students were evacuated to Ashkhabad (now Ashgabat, Turkm.), capital of the Turkmen Republic in Central Asia, where they resumed their studies and graduated in 1942. In 1945 they returned to Moscow, where Sakharov, accompanied by his wife, Klavdia Vikhireva, began his graduate work at the P.N. Lebedev Physics Institute of the Soviet Academy of Sciences (FIAN) under the direction of Igor Y. Tamm, earning his doctorate in two years.

In June 1948 Tamm was appointed to head a special research group at FIAN to investigate the possibility of building a thermonuclear bomb. Sakharov joined Tamm's group and, with his colleagues Vitaly Ginzburg and Yuri Romanov, worked on calculations produced by Yakov Zeldovich's group at the Institute of Chemical Physics. In March 1950 Sakharov arrived at the "Installation," located in what became the secret Soviet city of Sarov. There, under the scientific leadership of Yuly B. Khariton, members of the Tamm and Zeldovich groups worked on the thermonuclear bomb. A device built on Sakharov's "Layer Cake" model, small and light enough to be deliverable by airplane, was detonated on Aug. 12, 1953, with a yield of 400 kilotons. Sakharov was rewarded with full membership in the Soviet Academy of Sciences at age 32 and accorded the privileges of the Nomenklatura, or elite members of the Soviet Union.

After Tamm returned to Moscow in 1953, Sakharov assumed the duties of the theoretical department at the Installation. The following year saw the completion of a modern two-stage thermonuclear design, of which Sakharov was one of the originators. On Nov. 22, 1955, the Soviet Union successfully tested the design in a bomb detonated over the Semipalatinsk test site.

In the late 1950s Sakharov became concerned about the consequences of testing in the atmosphere, forseeing an eventual increased global death toll over time. In 1961 he went on record against plans for an atmospheric test of a 100-megaton thermonuclear bomb, fearing the hazards of widespread radioactive fallout. The bomb was tested at approximately half yield (58 megatons) on Oct. 30, 1961. Through these efforts, Sakharov began to adopt strong moral positions about the social responsibilities of scientists.

In May 1968 Sakharov finished his essay "Reflections on Progress, Peaceful Coexistence, and Intellectual Freedom," which first circulated as typewritten copies (samizdat) before being published in the West in the New York Times and elsewhere beginning in July. Sakharov warned of grave perils threatening the human race, called for nuclear arms reductions, predicted and endorsed the eventual convergence of communist and capitalist systems in a form of democratic socialism, and criticized the increasing repression of Soviet dissidents.

In 1975 Sakharov was awarded the Nobel Prize for Peace. The Soviet government reacted with extreme irritation and prevented Sakharov from leaving the country to attend the Nobel ceremony in Oslo. Sakharov's Nobel lecture was delivered by Yelena G. Bonner, a human rights activist whom he had married in 1972, after the death of his first wife. In 1980 the Soviet government stripped Sakharov of his honours and exiled him to the closed city of Gorky (now Nizhny Novgorod). In 1984 Bonner was convicted of anti-Soviet activities and was likewise confined to Gorky.

In 1985 Sakharov undertook a six-month hunger strike, eventually forcing the new Soviet leader Mikhail S. Gorbachev to grant Bonner permission to leave the country to have a heart bypass operation in the United States. During her six-month absence, she also met with Western leaders and others to focus concern on her husband's causes, and she wrote a book about their plight, entitled Alone Together (1986). Several months after she rejoined her husband, Gorbachev released Sakharov and Bonner from their exile, and in December 1986 they returned to Moscow and to a new Russia.

The final three years of Sakharov's life were filled with meetings with world leaders, press interviews, travel abroad, renewed contacts with his scientific colleagues, and the writing of his memoirs. In March 1989 he was elected to the First Congress of People's Deputies, representing the Academy of Sciences. Sakharov saw many of the causes for which he had fought and suffered become official policy under Gorbachev and his successors. He died on Dec. 14, 1989, in Moscow.

FRANCE

French scientists, such as Henri Becquerel, Marie and Pierre Curie, and Frédéric and Irène Joliot-Curie, made important contributions to 20th-century atomic physics. During World War II several French scientists participated in an Anglo-Canadian project in Canada, where eventually a heavy water reactor was built at Chalk River, Ont., in 1945.

On Oct. 18, 1945, the French Atomic Energy Commission (Commissariat à l'Énergie Atomique; CEA) was established by Gen. Charles de Gaulle with the objective of exploiting the scientific, industrial, and military potential of atomic energy. The military application of atomic energy did not begin until 1951. In July 1952 the National Assembly adopted a five-year plan with a primary goal of building plutonium production reactors. Work began on a reactor at Marcoule in the summer of 1954 and on a plutonium separating plant the following year.

On Dec. 26, 1954, the issue of proceeding with a French atomic bomb was raised at the cabinet level. The outcome was that Prime Minister Pierre Mendès-France launched a secret program to develop an atomic bomb. On Nov. 30, 1956, a protocol was signed specifying tasks the CEA and the Defense Ministry would perform. These included providing the plutonium, assembling a device, and preparing a test site. Key figures in developing the atomic bomb were Pierre Guillaumat, Gen. Charles Ailleret, and Yves Rocard. On July 22, 1958, de Gaulle, now president, set the date for the first atomic explosion to occur within the first three months of 1960. For de Gaulle especially, French attainment of the bomb symbolized independence and a role for France in geopolitical affairs. On Feb. 13, 1960, France detonated an atomic bomb from a 105-metre (344-foot) tower in the Sahara in what was then French Algeria. The plutonium implosion design had a yield of 60 to 70 kilotons, three times the yield of the atomic bomb dropped on Nagasaki, Japan. France carried out three more atmospheric and 13 additional underground tests in Algeria over the next six years before shifting its test site to the uninhabited atolls of Mururoa and Fangataufa in the Pacific Ocean. France conducted 194 tests in the Pacific from 1966 to 1996. These resulted in ever-improving fission, boosted-fission, and two-stage thermonuclear warheads for a variety of weapon systems, including aircraft bombs and missiles and land-based and sea-based ballistic missiles.

In 1997 an account of the French thermonuclear bomb program by physicist Pierre Billaud revealed details about the scientists who were involved in discovering the key concepts. Billaud was a director of the Centre de Limeil, the main French warhead design laboratory, located outside Paris, and from 1966 through 1968 he was one of the central figures in developing the French thermonuclear bomb.

According to Billaud, after the success of February 1960, the priority of the Direction des Applications Militaires—the part of the CEA responsible for the research, development, testing, and production of French nuclear warheads—was to adapt warheads for delivery by Mirage IV aircraft and to refine fission weapon designs. Thermonuclear bomb research was secondary until 1966, when de Gaulle, feeling the pressure that China might cross the thermonuclear threshold ahead of France, strongly urged the CEA to find a solution and set 1968 as a deadline. Work at Limeil and at other labs in the CEA complex was stepped up as scientists sought to discover the key concepts. Physicist Michel Carayol laid out what would be the fundamental idea of radiation implosion in an April 1967 paper, but neither he nor his colleagues were immediately convinced that it was the solution, and the search continued.

In late September 1967, Carayol's ideas were validated by an unlikely source, William Cook, who had overseen the British thermonuclear program in the mid-1950s. Cook, no doubt at his government's behest, verbally passed on the crucial information to the French embassy's military attaché in London. Presumably, the British provided this information for political reasons. British Prime Minister Harold Wilson was lobbying for the entry of the United Kingdom into the Common Market (European Economic Community), which was being blocked by de Gaulle.

Apparently, Wilson thought that sharing thermonuclear research with France would persuade de Gaulle to drop his country's veto. The ploy failed, however, as France again vetoed British entry on Nov. 27, 1967.

With confirmation now in hand about the right path, France quickly made plans to test Carayol's design at its Pacific test site. On Aug. 24, 1968 (14 months after the Chinese thermonuclear test), France entered the thermonuclear club with an explosion estimated at 2.6 megatons. On Sept. 8, 1968, Billaud supervised a second thermonuclear explosion, with a yield of 1.2 megatons.

CHINA

After winning the civil war in 1949, the new Chinese communist leadership viewed the United States—which backed the Nationalist Party of Chiang Kai-shek on Taiwan—as its main foreign threat. A series of conflicts and confrontations, beginning with the Korean War (1950–53), made China fear American military action and the possible use of U.S. nuclear weapons against China.

In response, on Jan. 15, 1955, Mao Zedong and the Chinese leadership decided to obtain their own nuclear arsenal. From 1955 to 1958 the Chinese were partially dependent on the Soviet Union for scientific and technological assistance, but from 1958 until the break in relations with the Soviet Union in 1960 they became more and more self-sufficient. Like the efforts of the other nuclear powers, China undertook the necessary large-scale mobilization of manpower and resources.

The major original facilities were built to produce and process uranium and plutonium at the Lanzhou Gaseous Diffusion Plant and the Jiuquan Atomic Energy Complex (JAEC), both in the northwestern province of Gansu. The reactor at JAEC began operation in 1967, and a large-scale reprocessing plant followed in April 1970. A design laboratory (called the Ninth Academy) was established at Haiyan, east of the Koko Nor (Blue Lake), Qinghai province, where initial production also took place. A test site at Lop Nur, in far northwestern China, was established in October 1959. Key figures in the Chinese bomb program included Wang Ganchang, Zhu Guangya, Deng Jiaxian, Peng Huanwu, Zhou Guangzhao, Yu Min, and Chen Nengkuan. Overall leadership and direction was provided by Marshal Nie Rongzhen, chairman of the State Science and Technology Commission from 1958 until 1967. As part of Mao's "Third Line" program to build a duplicate industrial infrastructure in remote regions of China as a strategic reserve in the event of war, a more modern nuclear complex was completed in the 1970s and '80s, supplementing and then replacing the original facilities.

Unlike the initial American, Soviet, and British tests, the first Chinese detonation—on Oct. 16, 1964—used uranium-235 in an implosion-type configuration that yielded 20 kilotons. Plutonium designs followed. Between 1964 and 1996 China conducted 23 atmospheric and 22 underground tests. This relatively limited number of tests resulted in a variety of fission and fusion warhead types with yields from a few kilotons to multimegatons.

China began to explore the feasibility of a thermonuclear bomb at the same time it initiated its atomic bomb program. More concrete plans to proceed were begun in December 1960, with the formation of a group by the Institute of Atomic Energy to do research on thermonuclear materials and reactions. In late 1963, after the design of the atomic bomb was complete, the Theoretical Department of the Ninth Academy, under the direction of Deng Jiaxian, was ordered to shift to thermonuclear work. Facilities were constructed to produce lithium-6 deuteride and other required components. By the end of 1965 the theoretical work for a multistage bomb had been completed, and manufacture of the test device was finished by the end of 1966. The first Chinese multistage fusion device, with a yield of three megatons, was detonated on June 17, 1967—this was only 32 months after China's first atomic test, the shortest span of the first five nuclear powers.

INDIA

India's nuclear policies and programs were somewhat idiosyncratic, compared with those of the other nuclear powers, and went through three distinct phases: from 1947 to 1974, from 1974 to 1998, and from 1998 into the 21st century. In 1948

Dwight D. Eisenhower delivering his Atoms for Peace speech to the United Nations General Assembly in New York City, December 1953. © United Nations/IAEA

the newly independent country passed an Atomic Energy Act, first introduced by Prime Minister Jawaharlal Nehru. The act established an Atomic Energy Commission (AEC), and Homi Bhabha was appointed its chairman. Bhabha had earned his doctorate in physics from the University of Cambridge and would be the central figure in shaping the Indian nuclear program, especially after becoming secretary of India's Department of Atomic Energy in 1954.

India took advantage of U.S. Pres. Dwight D. Eisenhower's Atoms for Peace program, first articulated in a UN speech in December 1953. The purpose of the program was to limit proliferation of nuclear weapons by offering technology for civilian use in exchange for a promise not to pursue military applications. The goal backfired because the dual uses of atomic energy are inherent in the technologies—a fact as well as a problem that was recognized at the birth of the atomic era and that continues to this day.

In 1955 Canada offered to build India a heavy water research reactor, and the United States supplied some of the heavy water. The reactor was built at Trombay, near Bombay (Mumbai), which would become the primary location of India's nuclear weapon program. (The facility was renamed the Bhabha Atomic Research Centre [BARC] after Bhabha died in 1966.) A reprocessing plant was built nearby to extract plutonium from spent fuel rods. The plant used the PUREX (*p*lutonium-*ur*anium-*ex*traction) chemical method developed by the United States—a process that had been made known to the world through the Atoms for Peace program. Hundreds of Indian scientists and engineers were trained in all aspects of nuclear technologies at laboratories and universities in the United States. By 1964 India had its first weapon-grade plutonium. Over the next decade, in parallel with peaceful uses of atomic energy, military research proceeded, while India rejected the 1968 Nuclear Non-proliferation Treaty.

On May 18, 1974, at the Pokhran test site on the Rajasthan Steppe, India, detonated a nuclear device with a yield later estimated to be less than 5 kilotons. (A figure of 12 kilotons was announced by India at the time.) India characterized the underground test as being for peaceful purposes, adding that it had no intentions of producing nuclear weapons. Among the key scientists and engineers directly involved were Homi Sethna, chairman of the AEC, Raja Ramanna, head of the BARC physics group, and Rajagopala Chidambaram, who headed a team that designed the plutonium core. Chidambaram later became chairman of the AEC and oversaw India's 1998 tests. Others mentioned with important roles were P.K. Iyengar, Satinder K. Sikka, Pranab R. Dastidar, Sekharipuram N.A. Seshadri, and Nagapattinam S. Venkatesan.

After 1974 India entered a second phase that lasted until 1998. During this period, India had the technical ability to produce nuclear weapons but maintained a policy of not deploying them. This ambivalent posture allowed India to continue its traditional stance of urging nuclear disarmament, while at the same time signaling that the military path was available to it if the situation warranted. Throughout the 1980s and '90s, Indian scientists continued to refine nuclear designs, including boosting and theoretical work on thermonuclear weapons. Modification of certain types of aircraft and advances in ballistic missile programs brought the prospect of a deployed nuclear force ever closer—a development driven in part by Pakistan's progress on its own nuclear weapons and by tensions with India's traditional adversary, China.

On May 11, 1998, India entered its third phase by detonating three devices simultaneously at the Pokhran test site. A press statement claimed that one was a fission device with a yield of about 12 kilotons, one was a thermonuclear device with a yield of 43 kilotons, and the third was a tactical device with a yield of 0.2 kiloton. On May 13 two more tactical devices were detonated, with reported yields of 0.2 and 0.6 kiloton. Western experts later disputed the size of the yields and whether any of them were thermonuclear bombs. U.S. intelligence concluded that the second stage failed to ignite. There was also speculation that one of the tests may have used reactor-grade plutonium. Among the key figures were Abdul Kalam, head of India's Defence Research and Development Organization, AEC chairman Rajagopala Chidambaram, BARC director Anil Kakodkar, and scientists M.S. Ramakumar, S.K. Gupta, and D.D. Sood.

Since 1998 India has moved forward with a vigorous program of developing weapon systems for the three branches of its armed forces. The emerging triad consists of the army's land-based ballistic missiles, the air force's air-delivered bombs, and the navy's sea-based ballistic missiles. India has not signed the 1996 Comprehensive Nuclear-Test-Ban Treaty (an extension of the 1963 Nuclear Test-Ban Treaty) and may need to test again.

PAKISTAN

Pakistan took advantage of the Atoms for Peace program by sending students abroad for training in nuclear technologies and by accepting an American-built research reactor, which began operation in 1965. Although its military nuclear research up to that point had been minimal, the situation soon changed. Pakistan's quest for the atomic bomb was in direct response to its defeat by India in December 1971, which resulted in East Pakistan becoming the independent country of Bangladesh. Immediately after the cease-fire, in late January 1972, the new Pakistani president, Zulfikar Ali Bhutto, convened a meeting of his top scientists and ordered them to build an atomic bomb. Bhutto, always suspicious of India, had wanted Pakistan to have the bomb for years and was now in a position to make it happen. Earlier he had famously said, "If India builds the bomb, we will eat grass or leaves, even go hungry, but we will get one of our own. We have no other choice."

Pakistan's route to the bomb was through the enrichment of uranium using high-speed gas centrifuges. A key figure was Abdul Qadeer Khan, a Pakistani scientist who had earned a doctorate in metallurgical engineering in Belgium. Beginning in May 1972, he began work at a laboratory in Amsterdam that was a subcontractor of a Dutch centrifuge company. In 1975 Khan abruptly left his job and returned to Pakistan with blueprints and photographs of centrifuges and contact information for dozens of companies that supplied the components. Working with the Pakistan Atomic Energy Commission, he founded a laboratory to build and operate a centrifuge plant in Kahuta using components that he had purchased from Europe and elsewhere.

By April 1978 Pakistan had produced enriched uranium, and four years later it had weapon-grade uranium. By the mid-1980s thousands of centrifuges were turning out enough uranium for making several atomic bombs per year, and by 1988, according to Pakistan Army Chief Gen. Mirza Aslam Beg, Pakistan had the capability of assembling a nuclear device. Khan likely had acquired the warhead design from China, apparently obtaining blueprints of an implosion device that was detonated in an October 1966 test, where uranium rather than plutonium was used. Khan would later use his contacts to form a vast black market network that sold or traded nuclear technology, centrifuges, and other items to North Korea, Iran, Libya, and possibly others.

In response to the Indian nuclear tests of May 1998, Pakistan claimed that it had successfully detonated five nuclear devices on May 28 in the Ros Koh Hills in the province of Balochistan and a sixth device two days later at a site 100 km (60 miles) to the southwest. As with the Indian nuclear claims, outside experts questioned the announced yields and even the number of tests.

A.Q. KHAN

Abdul Qadeer Khan was born on April 1, 1936, in Bhopal, India. In 1947, during Khan's childhood, India achieved independence from Britain, and Muslim areas in the east and west were partitioned to form the state of Pakistan. Khan immigrated to West Pakistan in 1952, and in 1960 he graduated from the University of Karachi with a degree in metallurgy. Over the next decade he pursued graduate studies abroad, first in West Berlin and then in Delft, Neth., where in 1967 he received a master's degree in metallurgy. In 1972 he earned a doctorate in metallurgical engineering from the Catholic University of Leuven in Belgium.

In the spring of 1972 Khan was hired by Physical Dynamics Research Laboratory, a subcontractor of the Dutch partner of URENCO. URENCO, a consortium of British, German, and Dutch companies, was established in 1971 to research and develop uranium enrichment through the use of ultracentrifuges, which are centrifuges that operate at extremely high speeds. Khan was granted a low-level security clearance, but, through lax oversight, he gained access to a full range of information on ultracentrifuge technology and visited the Dutch plant at Almelo many times.

Khan was heavily influenced by events back home, notably Pakistan's humiliating defeat in a brief war with India in 1971, the subsequent loss of East Pakistan through the creation of a new independent country, Bangladesh, and India's test of a nuclear explosive device in May 1974. On Sept. 17, 1974, Khan wrote to Pakistan's prime minister, Zulfikar Ali Bhutto, offering his assistance in preparing an atomic bomb. In the letter he offered the opinion that the uranium route to the bomb, using centrifuges for enrichment, was better than the plutonium path (already under way in Pakistan), which relied on nuclear reactors and reprocessing.

Bhutto met Khan in December 1974 and encouraged him to do everything he could to help Pakistan attain the bomb. Over the next year Khan stole drawings of centrifuges and assembled a list of mainly European suppliers where parts could be procured. On Dec. 15, 1975, he left the Netherlands for Pakistan, accompanied by his wife and two daughters and carrying his blueprint copies and suppliers list.

In mid-1976, at Bhutto's direction, Khan founded a research laboratory for the purpose of developing a uranium-enrichment capability. Khan's base of operations was in Kahuta, 50 km (30 miles) southeast of Islamabad; there Khan developed prototype centrifuges based on German designs and used his suppliers list to import essential components from Swiss, Dutch, British, and German companies, among others.

In the early 1980s Pakistan acquired from China the blueprints of a nuclear weapon that used a uranium implosion design that the Chinese had successfully tested in 1966. It is generally believed that the Chinese tested a derivative design for the Pakistanis on May 26, 1990. Khan, having satisfied Pakistan's needs for its own uranium weapon, began in the mid-1980s to create front companies in Dubayy, Malaysia, and elsewhere, and through these entities he covertly sold or traded centrifuges, components, designs, and expertise in an extensive black-market network. The customers included Iran, which went on to build a uranium-enrichment complex based on the Pakistani model. Khan visited North Korea at least 13 times and is suspected of having transferred enrichment technology to that country. Libya, supplied by Khan, embarked upon a nuclear weapons program until it was interrupted by the United States in 2003.

On Jan. 31, 2004, Khan was arrested for transferring nuclear technology to other countries. He read a statement on Pakistani television taking full responsibility for his operations and absolving the military and government of any involvement—a claim that many nuclear experts found difficult to believe. The next day he was pardoned by Pakistan's president, Pervez Musharraf, but he was held under house arrest until 2009. Khan's critics, particularly in the West, expressed dismay at such lenient treatment of a man whom one observer called "the greatest nuclear proliferator of all time." For many Pakistanis, however, Khan remains a symbol of pride, a hero whose contribution strengthened Pakistan's national security against India.

A single Western seismic measurement for May 28 suggested the yield was on the order of 9 to 12 kilotons rather than the official Pakistani announcement of 40 to 45 kilotons. For the May 30 nuclear test, Western estimates were from 4 to 6 kilotons rather than the official Pakistani figure of 15 to 18 kilotons. Nevertheless, there was no doubt that Pakistan had joined the nuclear club and that, with various ballistic and cruise missile programs under way, it was in an arms race with India.

ISRAEL

Israel was the sixth country to acquire nuclear weapons, though it has never officially acknowledged the fact. Israel's declared policy regarding nuclear weapons was first articulated in the mid-1960s by Prime Minister Levi Eshkol with the ambiguous statement, "Israel will not be the first state to introduce nuclear weapons into the region."

The Israeli nuclear program began in the mid-1950s. Three key figures are credited with its founding. Israel's first prime minister, David Ben-Gurion, made the decision to undertake a nuclear weapons program. From behind the scenes, Shimon Peres, director-general of the Ministry of Defense, selected personnel, allocated resources, and became the chief administrator of the entire project. Scientist Ernst David Bergmann, the first chairman of Israel's Atomic Energy Commission, provided early technical guidance. Crucial to Israel's success was collaboration with France. Through Peres's diplomatic efforts, in October 1957 France agreed to sell Israel a reactor and an underground reprocessing plant, which was built near the town of Dimona in the Negev desert. Many Israeli scientists and engineers were trained at French nuclear facilities. In another secret agreement, signed in 1959, Norway agreed to supply via Britain 20 metric tons of heavy water for the reactor.

In June 1958 a new research and development authority named RAFAEL (a Hebrew acronym for the Armaments Development Authority) was established within the Ministry of Defense to assist in the weaponization side of the project, along with the organization of the Dimona Nuclear Research Centre to be built in the Negev. Ground was broken at Dimona in late 1958 or early 1959. By 1965 the first plutonium had been produced, and on the eve of the Six-Day War in June 1967 Israel had two or three assembled devices. Over the years the Dimona facility was upgraded to produce more plutonium. Other scientists known to have contributed to the Israeli nuclear program include Jenka Ratner, Avraham Hermoni, Israel Dostrovsky, Yosef Tulipman, and Shalheveth Freier.

Additional details about the Israeli nuclear program and arsenal have come to light as a result of revelations by Mordechai Vanunu, a technician who worked at Dimona from 1977 to 1985. Before leaving his job, Vanunu took dozens of photographs of Dimona's most secret areas, as well as of plutonium components, of a full-scale model of a thermonuclear bomb, and of work on tritium that implied Israel might have built boosted weapons. He provided an extensive account of what he knew to the London *Sunday Times*, which published a story, "Inside Dimona, Israel's Nuclear Bomb Factory," on Oct. 5, 1986. Five days before the article was published, Vanunu was abducted in Rome by the Mossad (one of Israel's intelligence agencies),

taken to Israel, tried, and sentenced to 18 years in prison. He spent 10 years of his prison term in solitary confinement. Later, American weapon designers analyzed the photographs and concluded that Israel's nuclear arsenal was much larger than previously thought (perhaps between 100 and 200 weapons) and that Israel was capable of building a neutron bomb, a low-yield thermonuclear device that reduces blast and maximizes the radiation effect. (Israel may have tested a neutron bomb over the southern Indian Ocean on Sept. 22, 1979.) At the turn of the 21st century, the U.S. Defense Intelligence Agency estimated that Israel had 60 to 80 nuclear weapons.

SOUTH AFRICA

South Africa is the only country to have produced nuclear weapons and then voluntarily dismantled and destroyed them. On March 24, 1993, South African Pres. F.W. de Klerk informed the country's parliament that South Africa had secretly produced six nuclear devices and had subsequently dismantled them prior to acceding to the Nuclear Nonproliferation Treaty on July 10, 1991.

In 1974 South Africa decided to develop a nuclear explosive capability allegedly for peaceful purposes, but after 1977 the program acquired military applications in response to growing fears about communist expansion on South Africa's borders. The weapon program was highly compartmentalized, with probably no more than 10 people knowing all of the details, though about 1,000 persons were involved in different aspects. J.W. de Villiers is thought to have been in charge of developing the explosive. By 1978 the first quantity of highly enriched uranium was produced at the Y-Plant at Valindaba, next to the Pelindaba Nuclear Research Centre, 19 km (12 miles) west of Pretoria. The enrichment method used was an "aerodynamic" process, developed by South African scientists, in which a mixture of uranium hexafluoride and hydrogen gas is compressed and injected at high speeds into tubes that are spun to separate the isotopes.

A fission gun-assembly design, similar to the Little Boy bomb dropped on Hiroshima, was chosen. It has been estimated that the South African version contained 55 kg (121 pounds) of highly enriched uranium and had a yield of 10 to 18 kilotons. In 1985 South Africa decided to build seven weapons. Six were completed, and the seventh was partially built by November 1989, when the government ceased production. The nuclear and nonnuclear components were stored separately. The two subcritical pieces of highly enriched uranium for each weapon were kept in vaults at the Kentron Circle (later renamed Advena) facility, about 16 km (10 miles) east of Pelindaba, where they had been fabricated. When fully assembled, the weapon weighed about one ton, was 1.8 metres (6 feet) long and 63.5 cm (25 inches) in diameter, and could have been deliverable by a modified Buccaneer bomber. However, the bombs were never integrated into the armed forces, and no offensive attack plans were ever drawn up for their use.

The government decision to disarm was made in November 1989, and over the next 18 months the devices were dismantled, the uranium was made unsuitable for weapon use, the components and technical documents were destroyed, and the Y-Plant was decommissioned. The International Atomic Energy Agency (IAEA) inspected South Africa's facilities beginning in November 1991, and it eventually concluded that the weapons program had been terminated and the devices dismantled.

According to South African officials, the weapons were never meant to be used militarily. Rather, they were intended to force Western governments, particularly the United States, to come to South Africa's aid if it were ever threatened. The plan was for South Africa first to inform the West covertly that it had the bomb. If that failed, South Africa would either publicly declare it had a nuclear arsenal or detonate a nuclear bomb in a deep shaft at the Vastrap test site in the Kalahari to demonstrate the fact.

NORTH KOREA

Little authoritative information has been made available about the North Korean nuclear program. Western intelligence agencies and scholars provide most of what is known. The threat of a nuclear attack by the United States both during and after the Korean War may have spurred North Korea's Kim Il-sung to launch a nuclear weapons program of his own, which began with help from the Soviet Union in the 1960s. China provided various kinds of support over the next two decades, and Abdul Qadeer Khan of Pakistan apparently provided uranium enrichment equipment and warhead designs.

The centre of North Korea's nuclear program is at Yŏngbyŏn, about 100 km (60 miles) north of the capital of P'yŏngyang. Its major facilities include a reactor that became operational in 1986, a reprocessing plant, and a fuel fabrication plant. The 5-megawatt reactor is capable of producing about 6 kg (13 pounds) of plutonium per year. The U.S. Central Intelligence Agency concluded in the early 1990s that North Korea had effectively joined the other nuclear powers by building one or possibly two weapons from plutonium that had been produced prior to 1992.

From 1994 to 2002, as a result of an agreement with the United States, the North Korean nuclear program was effectively frozen, as its nuclear reactor was shut down. In October 2002 the United States accused North Korea of having resumed its military nuclear program, and in response P'yŏngyang announced that it would withdraw from the Nuclear Non-proliferation Treaty—the only country ever to do so. North Korea's reactor was restarted, and more plutonium was extracted. Estimates vary on how much plutonium was subsequently separated and how many bombs were made from it.

One assessment calculated that some 28 to 50 kg (62 to 110 pounds) of plutonium were produced for weapon use. Assuming each weapon contained 4 to 5 kg (9 to 11 pounds), this would be enough for 5 to 12 weapons. Much depended on the technical capability of North Korean designers and the desired yield of the weapons.

On Oct. 9, 2006, North Korea conducted an underground nuclear test in its northeastern Hamgyŏng Mountains. Western experts estimated the yield as approximately one kiloton, much lower than the initial tests of the other nuclear powers. Chinese officials said that P'yŏngyang informed them in advance that they planned for a test of four kilotons. Over the following years, international pressure and concentrated diplomacy by the United States and other countries in the region attempted to halt North Korea's nuclear program. This did not prevent the country from conducting another, more powerful underground nuclear test in May 2009.

OTHER COUNTRIES

In the decades following 1945, several countries initiated nuclear research and development programs but for one reason or another decided not to proceed to the next stage and produce actual weapons. For example, Sweden had a vigorous nuclear weapons research program for 20 years, from the late 1940s to the late 1960s, before the government decided not to go forward. Switzerland, too, examined the possibility but did not proceed very far. Even today several technologically advanced countries, such as Japan and Germany, are sometimes referred to as virtual nuclear countries because they could fabricate a weapon fairly quickly with their technical knowledge and domestic stocks of separated plutonium.

Several other countries have had fledging nuclear weapons programs that were abandoned through outside pressure, rapprochement with an adversary, or unilateral decisions not to acquire a nuclear capability. Representative of this category are Taiwan, Argentina, Brazil, Libya, and Iraq. Iran meanwhile has acquired the means to produce enriched uranium despite concerns expressed by the IAEA and the United Nations Security Council that this material may be used to produce nuclear weapons. The programs of these countries are described in turn below.

TAIWAN

The purpose and scale of Taiwan's program remains unclear, though a few details have emerged. After China's 1964 nuclear test, Taiwan launched a program to produce weapon-grade nuclear material—purchasing a small heavy water research reactor from Canada and various facilities from other countries. By the mid-1970s the United States and the IAEA began to apply pressure on Taiwan to abandon its program, and Taiwan eventually acceded.

ARGENTINA AND BRAZIL

Argentina and Brazil were engaged in competing programs to develop nuclear weapons, mostly under their respective military regimes, in the late 1970s and throughout the 1980s. The competition ended in the early 1990s as both countries canceled their programs, agreed to inspections, and signed the Nuclear Non-proliferation Treaty.

LIBYA

Beginning in the early 1980s, Libya undertook a secret nuclear weapons program in violation of its commitments to the Nuclear Non-proliferation Treaty. Libya's program accelerated after 2000, when Libya began to import parts for 10,000 centrifuges in order to enrich uranium—though few machines were ever assembled or made operational. In October 2003 the U.S. Navy intercepted and diverted a German freighter bound for Tripoli that was carrying thousands of centrifuge components, which had originated in Abdul Qadeer Khan's black market network. In December 2003 Libyan leader Muammar al-Qaddafi publicly stated that all WMD programs would be terminated and that inspectors would be allowed to confirm their elimination. Libyan officials also admitted that they had obtained blueprints for a nuclear warhead design from Khan, though the warhead would have been too large to fit on a Libyan missile. Experts who analyzed the Libyan program concluded that it was in its early stages, not well organized, understaffed, incomplete, and many years away from building an atomic bomb.

IRAQ

Though a signatory to the Nuclear Nonproliferation Treaty, Iraq began a secret nuclear weapons program in the 1970s, using the claim of civilian applications as a cover. In 1976 France agreed to sell Iraq a research reactor (called Osirak or Tammuz-1) that used weapon-grade uranium as the fuel. Iraq imported hundreds of tons of various forms of uranium from Portugal, Niger, and Brazil, sent numerous technicians abroad for training, and in 1979 contracted to purchase a plutonium separation facility from Italy. Iraq's program was dealt a setback

Remains of a facility used for Iraq's clandestine nuclear weapons program. The IAEA (International Atomic Energy Agency) examined the site following the Persian Gulf War (1990–91). © IAEA Action Team

when Israeli aircraft bombed the Osirak reactor on June 7, 1981, demolishing the reactor's core. Over the next decade, several methods of enriching uranium were undertaken by Iraq, but the country's ambitious plans were never realized, and by the end of the Persian Gulf War (1990–91) only a few grams of weapon-grade nuclear material had been produced.

UN inspectors uncovered a sizable Iraqi clandestine biological weapons program after Pres. Saddam Hussein's son-in-law, Hussein Kamil, who headed the program, defected in August 1995. In 1998 Saddam forced the UN inspectors out, leading to growing suspicions that WMD programs were once again being pursued. The inspectors returned in November 2002 but did not find any evidence of resuscitated programs before the beginning of the Iraq War on March 20, 2003. No WMD were discovered following American occupation of Iraq.

IRAN

In the late 1970s the United States obtained intelligence indicating that Mohammad Reza Shah Pahlavi had established a clandestine nuclear weapons program, though Iran had signed the Nuclear Non-proliferation Treaty in 1968. The Islamic Revolution of 1979 and the Iran-Iraq War (1980–88) that followed interrupted this program, but by the late 1980s new efforts were under way, especially with the assistance of Abdul

Qadeer Khan, who sold Iran gas centrifuge technology and provided training to Iranian scientists and engineers. The Iranians also began secretly to construct a number of nuclear facilities in violation of their safeguards agreements with the IAEA. In 2002 an Iranian opposition group in Paris revealed the existence of a uranium enrichment facility at Naṭanz and a heavy water plant at Arāk, spurring the IAEA to take action.

Iran had contracted with Russia in 1995 to finish a nuclear power plant begun by West Germany in the mid-1970s at Būshehr, raising international concerns that it could be used as part of a weapons program. Beginning in February 2003, IAEA inspectors made many visits to suspected facilities and raised questions about their purpose, and in September 2005 the IAEA's Governing Board found Iran in noncompliance with its safeguards obligations. Iran claimed that it was pursuing nuclear technologies for peaceful civilian purposes, which are legal under the Nuclear Non-proliferation Treaty, but many believed that Iran was creating a nuclear infrastructure in order eventually to build a nuclear weapon.

By 2005 the reactor at Būshehr was essentially complete. Aside from the fresh reactor fuel supplied by Russia, by 2008 Iran had produced enough low-enrichment uranium (less than 5 percent uranium-235) at its enrichment facility to fuel a single implosion-type fission weapon—if, that is, the low-enriched uranium were further enriched to about 90 percent uranium-235. However, enrichment beyond 5 percent uranium-235 would place Iran in violation of its safeguards obligations, and the enrichment process would likely be detected by the IAEA's inspectors before the highly enriched uranium could be assembled into a deliverable nuclear weapon. Official and expert opinions varied on when Iran might have the capability of building a nuclear bomb if it should choose to do so, with estimates ranging from 2015 to 2020. In any case, in 2010 it became apparent that a sophisticated computer worm called Stuxnet had infected computerized control systems in Iran's nuclear program and had rendered enrichment centrifuges temporarily unusable. No country or organization claimed responsibility for the sabotage, though Iran accused the United States and Israel.

CHAPTER 4

NUCLEAR STRATEGY DURING THE COLD WAR

Nuclear strategy is no different from any other form of strategy in that it involves relating military means to political ends. In this case, however, the military means in question have been so powerful and destructive that it has been doubted whether any worthwhile political purpose could be served by their use. On the one hand, it has been questioned whether any country with pretensions to civilization could unleash such a devastating force as nuclear weapons. On the other hand, it has been noted that their use against an opponent similarly endowed would result in an equally ruinous retaliation. The central issue for nuclear strategy, therefore, is less how to win and wage a nuclear war than whether by preparing to do so it is possible to create a deterrent effect. The minimum objective would be to deter another's nuclear use; the maximum, to deter any aggression on the grounds that any hostilities might create the extreme circumstances in which the restraints on nuclear use would fall away.

This maximum objective, which was the one adopted by both superpowers during the Cold War period, required close attention to the links with more conventional strategy and to the wider political context, including alliance formation and disintegration. However, nuclear strategists paid little attention to this wider context because of the East-West conflict's remarkable continuity, with two alliances each dominated by a superpower—the North Atlantic Treaty Organization (NATO) by the United States and the Warsaw Pact by the Soviet Union. Although attempts to reproduce these alliances in continents other than Europe met with scant success, their stability within Europe meant that they were virtually taken for granted.

In the summer of 1945, British Prime Minister Winston Churchill (left), U.S. Pres. Harry Truman (centre), and Soviet Premier Josef Stalin met at the Potsdam Conference in Germany to discuss the new order in Europe after World War II. © AP Images

Nuclear strategy then became associated with more technical questions relating to the capabilities of various weapons systems and the range of potential forms of interaction with those of an enemy under hypothetical scenarios.

THE ATOMIC BOMB AND AMERICAN STRATEGIC THOUGHT

The first successful test of the atomic bomb took place in New Mexico in July 1945 as the leaders of Britain, the Soviet Union, and the United States met at the Potsdam Conference to discuss the shape of the postwar world. This context coloured the early American appreciation of the potential foreign-policy role of the new weapons, with the result that nuclear strategy thereafter became bound up with the twists and turns of the Cold War between East and West.

However, the decision to actually use the bomb against Japan reflected the more immediate urge to end the war as soon as possible and certainly before it became necessary to mount an invasion of the mainland. The atomic bombing of Hiroshima and Nagasaki in August 1945 was a means of shocking Japan into surrender. The choice of civilian rather than purely military targets, and the consequent immense loss of life, reflected the brutalizing experience of the massive air raids that had become commonplace during the war. Afterward it was assumed that any future atomic bombing would also be against cities. As weapons of terror, they appeared to have brought 20th-century trends in warfare to their logical conclusion.

The first nuclear weapons were in the range of other munitions (the bomb that destroyed Hiroshima was equivalent to the load of some 200 B-29 bombers); also, at least initially, the weapons were scarce. The key development introduced by atomic bombs was less in the scale of their destructive power than in their efficiency. By the start of the 1950s, though, this situation had been transformed by two related developments. The first was the breaking of the U.S. monopoly by the Soviet Union, which conducted its first atomic bomb test in August 1949. Once two could play the nuclear game, the rules had to be changed. Anyone who thought of initiating nuclear war would henceforth need to consider the possibility of retaliation.

The second development followed from the first. In an effort to extend its effective nuclear superiority, the United States produced thermonuclear bombs, based on the principles of nuclear fusion rather than fission, upon which the atomic bombs were based. This made possible weapons with no obvious limits to their destructive potential. Opposition to this development by influential nuclear scientists, such as Robert Oppenheimer, was disregarded by Pres. Harry S. Truman on the grounds that the Soviet Union would not suffer from any comparable moral inhibitions.

This move was not matched by a pronounced nuclear bias in U.S. strategy. The weapons were still scarce, and it seemed only a matter of time before any advantages accruing to the United States through its lead would be neutralized as the Soviet Union caught up. The Truman administration assumed that the introduction of thermonuclear weapons would extend the time available to the United States and its allies (including NATO) to build up conventional forces to match those of the Soviet Union and its satellites. A series of events, from the Berlin blockade of 1948 to the Korean War of 1950–53, had convinced the United States that the communists were prepared to use military means to pursue their political ambitions and that this could be countered only by a major program of Western rearmament.

MASSIVE RETALIATION

The administration of Pres. Dwight D. Eisenhower, which came to power in January 1953, saw things differently. It reflected on the frustrating experience of the inconclusive conventional war fought in Korea and wondered why the West had not made more use of its nuclear superiority. Eisenhower was also extremely worried about the economic burden of conventional rearmament. Assigning a greater priority to nuclear weapons provided the opportunity to scale down expensive conventional forces. By this time the nuclear arsenal was becoming more plentiful and more powerful.

The strategy that emerged from these considerations became known as "massive retaliation," following a speech made by U.S. Secretary of State John Foster Dulles in January 1954, when he declared that in the future a U.S. response to aggression would be "at places and with means of our own choosing." This doctrine was interpreted as threatening nuclear attack against targets in the Soviet Union and China in response to conventional aggression anywhere in the world.

JOHN FOSTER DULLES

John Foster Dulles was born on Feb. 25, 1888, in Washington, D.C., and was educated in the public schools of Watertown, N.Y., where his father served as a Presbyterian minister. A brilliant student, he attended Princeton and George Washington universities and the Sorbonne, and in 1911 he entered the New York law firm of Sullivan and Cromwell, specializing in international law. By 1927 he was head of the firm.

Dulles started his diplomatic career in 1907 when, aged 19, he accompanied his grandfather John Foster, a former secretary of state who was now representing China, to the second international peace conference at The Hague. At 30 years of age Dulles was named by Pres. Woodrow Wilson as legal counsel to the U.S. delegation to the Versailles Peace Conference, at the end of World War I, and afterward he served as a member of the war reparations commission.

In World War II, Dulles helped prepare the United Nations charter at Dumbarton Oaks, in Washington, D.C., and in 1945 served as a senior adviser at the San Francisco United Nations conference. When it became apparent that a

John Foster Dulles. Hulton Archive/ Getty Images

peace treaty with Japan acceptable to the United States could not be concluded with the participation of the Soviet Union, Pres. Harry Truman and his secretary of state, Dean Acheson, assigned to Dulles the difficult task of personally negotiating and concluding the treaty. Dulles traveled to the capitals of many of the nations involved, and in 1951 the previously agreed to treaty was signed in San Francisco by Japan and 48 other nations. In 1949 Dulles was appointed U.S. senator from New York to fill a vacancy, but he served for only four months before being defeated in the 1950 election.

Dulles viewed his appointment as secretary of state by President Eisenhower, in January 1953, as a mandate to originate foreign policy. "The State Department," Dulles once told an aide, "can only keep control of foreign policy as long as we have ideas." A man bent on realizing his ideas, he was an assiduous planner, and, once he enjoyed President Eisenhower's complete confidence, policy planning flourished during his administration.

Three factors determined Dulles' foreign policy: his profound detestation of Communism, which was in part based on his deep religious faith; his powerful personality, which often insisted on leading rather than following public opinion; and his strong belief, as an international lawyer, in the value of treaties. Of the three, passionate hostility to Communism was the leitmotiv of his policy. Wherever he went, he carried with him Joseph Stalin's Problems of Leninism and impressed upon his aides the need to study it as a blueprint for conquest similar to Adolf Hitler's Mein Kampf. He seemed to derive personal satisfaction from pushing the Soviet Union to the brink. In fact, in 1956 he wrote in a magazine article that "if you are scared to go to the brink, you are lost."

But Dulles could be equally intransigent with the allies of the United States. His insistence upon the establishment of the European Defense Community (EDC) threatened to polarize the free world, when in 1953 he announced that failure to ratify EDC by France would result in an "agonizing reappraisal" of the United States' relations with France. That expression, and Dulles' announcement in a Paris speech that the United States would react with "massive nuclear retaliation" to any Soviet aggression, found a permanent place in the vocabulary of U.S. foreign policy.

Dulles' detractors in the United States and abroad viewed him as harsh, inflexible, and a tactician, rather than an architect of international diplomacy. But President Eisenhower ignored all criticisms. He said of his secretary of state, "He is one of the truly great men of our time." Whatever their opinion of the man and his policies, many leading statesmen of the non-Communist nations have credited his firmness with having checkmated Communist Cold War strategy. Seriously ill with cancer, Dulles resigned his Cabinet position on April 15, 1959. Shortly before he died, on May 24, 1959, in Washington, he was awarded the Medal of Freedom.

Massive retaliation was widely criticized. In the United States the Democratic Party, whose policy under Truman was being reversed—and the army and navy, whose budgets were being cut at the expense of the air force's Strategic Air Command—charged that it placed undue reliance on nuclear threats, which would become less credible as Soviet nuclear strength grew. If a limited challenge developed anywhere around the Sino-Soviet periphery (the two communist giants were seen to constitute a virtual monolith) and the United States neglected its own conventional forces, then a choice would have to be faced between "suicide or surrender."

FIRST AND SECOND STRIKES

Massive retaliation was also criticized for failing to appreciate possible areas of Soviet superiority. This criticism grew after the Soviet Union demonstrated its technological prowess by successfully launching the first artificial Earth satellite (Sputnik 1) in October 1957, not long after it had also made the first tests of an ICBM, the SS-6. Concern grew that the Soviet Union was outpacing the United States in missile production and thereby leading to a "missile gap." (It might have been argued that after a certain level of destructive capability had been reached by both sides, an effective stalemate would be reached and extra weapons would make little difference, promising only, as British Prime Minister Winston Churchill put it, to make "the rubble bounce.")

However, by this time nuclear strategy was becoming much more sophisticated. With the RAND Corporation, a think tank based in Santa Monica, Calif., taking the lead, new analytical techniques were being developed. These were often drawn from engineering and economics, rather than the more traditional strategic disciplines of history and politics. In a celebrated RAND study of the mid-1950s, a team led by Albert Wohlstetter demonstrated that the air bases of the Strategic Air Command could be vulnerable to a surprise attack, after which retaliation would be impossible, a situation that would expose the United States and its allies to Soviet blackmail.

A devastating surprise attack was considered possible because, with improved guidance systems, nuclear weapons were becoming more precise. Therefore, it was not inevitable that they would be used solely in countervalue strikes against easily targeted political and economic centres; instead, it was just as likely that they would be used in counterforce strikes against military targets. A successful counterforce attack that rendered retaliation impossible—known as a "first strike"—would be strategically decisive. If, however, the attacked nation possessed sufficient forces to survive an attempted first strike with retaliatory weapons intact, then it would have what became known as a second-strike capability.

Other strategists, such as Thomas Schelling, warned that if both sides sought a first-strike capability, this could lead to an extremely unstable situation, especially during a period of high political tension when both were nervous as to the other's intentions. If it was feared that an enemy first strike was imminent, then there would be powerful pressures to attack first, and if the enemy recognized these pressures, then that would encourage him to get in his strike. Schelling described this as the "reciprocal fear of surprise attack."

On the other hand, if both sides were confident of their second-strike capabilities, then there would be considerable stability, as there would be no premium attached to unleashing nuclear hostilities. The benefits of a mutual second-strike capability led to the concept of arms control, by which potential adversaries would put less priority on simply lowering their force levels (as advocated by proponents of disarmament) and more on removing incentives to take the military initiative in the event of a severe crisis.

MUTUAL ASSURED DESTRUCTION

In the event, technological developments supported the second strike. Initially, long-range bombers had to be kept on continual alert to prevent them from being eliminated in a surprise attack. When ICBMs moved into full production in the early 1960s with such systems as the U.S. Titan and Minuteman I and the Soviet SS-7 and SS-8, they were placed in hardened underground silos so that it would require an unlikely direct hit to destroy them. Even less vulnerable were SLBMs such as the U.S. Polaris and the Soviet SS-N-5 and SS-N-6, which could take full advantage of the ocean expanses to hide from enemy attack.

Meanwhile, attempts to develop effective defenses against nuclear attack proved futile. The standards for antiaircraft defense in the nuclear age had to be much higher than for conventional air raids, since any penetration of the defensive screen would threaten the defender with catastrophe. Progress was made, using surface-to-air missiles (SAMs) such as the U.S. Nike series, in developing defenses against bombers, but the move to ICBMs, with their minimal warning time before impact, appeared to render the defensive task hopeless. Then, during the 1960s, advances in radars and long-range SAMs promised a breakthrough in antiballistic missile defense, but by the early 1970s these in turn had been countered by improvements in offensive missiles—notably multiple independently targeted reentry vehicles (MIRVs), which could swamp any defenses. (The first MIRVed ICBMs were the U.S. Minuteman III and the Soviet SS-17.)

Measures of civil defense, which could offer little protection to the civilian populace against nuclear explosions and, at best, only some chance of avoiding exposure to nuclear fallout, also appeared hopeless in the face of the overwhelming destructive power being accumulated by both sides.

By the mid-1960s fears had eased of a technological arms race that might encourage either side to unleash a surprise attack. For the foreseeable future each side could eliminate the other as a modern industrial state. Robert McNamara, the U.S. secretary of defense for much of that decade, argued that so long as the two superpowers had confidence in their capacity for mutual assured destruction—an ability to impose "unacceptable damage," defined as 25 percent of population and 50 percent of industry—the relationship between the two would be stable.

The need to maintain strategic stability influenced the Strategic Arms Limitation Talks (SALT), which began in 1969 and became the centrepiece of Pres. Richard M. Nixon's policy of détente with the Soviet Union. In 1972, with the Anti-Ballistic Missile (ABM) Treaty, the two sides agreed to ban nationwide antiballistic missile systems, thereby confirming the primacy of the offense. Attempts to consolidate the strategic standoff with a treaty limiting offensive weapons proved more difficult. (In 1972 only an interim freeze had been agreed upon.) The second round of talks was guided mainly by the concept of parity, by which a broad equality in destructive power would be confirmed. However, the difficulty in comparing the two nuclear arsenals, which differed in important respects, resulted in long and complex negotiations. A treaty called SALT II was agreed on in June 1979, but by this time détente was in decline, and it was dealt a final blow with the Soviet intervention in Afghanistan at the end of that year. In addition, the strategic underpinnings of arms control had been undermined by a growing dissatisfaction in the United States with the principles of mutual assured destruction.

ALTERNATIVES TO ASSURED DESTRUCTION

Critics found the condition of mutual assured destruction—which had become known by its acronym MAD—alarming. If MAD failed to deter, then any war would soon lead to genocide. In addition, if the threat of retaliating with nuclear weapons was used to deter only nuclear attack, then the value of nuclear threats in deterring conventional aggression would be lost. In principle, this could undermine the commitments made to allies to use nuclear weapons on their behalf if they faced such aggression.

Particularly alarming was evidence that the nuclear strategy of the Soviet Union envisaged using nuclear weapons in a traditional military manner much as if they were conventional weapons—that is, at most to obtain a decisive military advantage in a conflict and at the very least to reduce the damage that an enemy might do to Soviet territory (if necessary, by launching preemptive strikes). During the negotiations that led to SALT II, critics also argued that the momentum behind the Soviet ICBM program, in combination with improved guidance systems that gave unprecedented accuracy to MIRVed missiles, had opened a "window of vulnerability" in the U.S. deterrent force. They expressed concern that the Soviet Union, by deploying the SS-17, SS-18, and SS-19 ICBMs, was building a force of such size and accuracy that just a portion of it could attack and destroy the U.S. Minuteman and Titan

ICBM force without killing huge numbers of civilians. Although this would not be a true first strike, since U.S. bombers and submarines could retaliate, these latter delivery systems were not accurate enough to produce an equivalent counterforce attack against Soviet missile silos. Instead, the United States would be forced to escalate the war by retaliating against cities. This repugnant act would be of no strategic value, however, because the rest of the untouched Soviet missile force would then be used to wipe out U.S. cities. The United States, therefore, would have placed itself in a position in which it would have to choose between surrender and slaughter.

The realism of this scenario may be doubted, given that no attack against United States ICBMs would be accurate enough to avoid massive civilian destruction; therefore, the Soviet Union could be certain that the United States would feel little repugnance at retaliating against Soviet cities. Nonetheless, it was used to criticize SALT II, a complicated treaty that offered few means of verification and did little to interfere with the Soviet ICBM program. It was also used to argue for the development of U.S. ICBMs comparable to the Soviet systems.

The first formal break with assured destruction came when Secretary of Defense James Schlesinger announced in 1974 that future U.S. nuclear targeting would be geared to selective strikes and not just the sort of massive attacks suggested by the philosophy of mutual assured destruction. Although Pres.

Jimmy Carter's secretary of defense, Harold Brown, was skeptical that either side would actually find such sophisticated nuclear strikes possible, he accepted the need to develop a range of targeting options to convince the Soviet Union that it could not gain the upper hand by such methods. This was the main theme of the "countervailing" strategy announced in 1980.

Ronald W. Reagan came to office the next year with a much more radical critique of MAD, and his presidency was devoted to attempts to escape from its constraints. Initially, this took the form of a search for offensive nuclear operations that would enable the United States to prevail in a protracted war with the Soviet Union, rather than just countervail. It involved upgrading the old civil-defense systems and deploying the MX, an experimental ICBM originally designed to survive a first strike through some form of mobile deployment. Neither of these ideas was politically popular. In the end, civil defense was rejected as impossible, and the MX (later named the Peacekeeper missile) was deployed in Minuteman silos and in only a fraction of the originally proposed numbers.

In March 1983 Reagan announced the start of a second search for a means to escape from MAD. This time it was for a defensive system that could intercept ballistic missiles. Reagan spoke of his preference for protecting lives rather than avenging them, and of the possibility of rendering nuclear weapons "impotent and obsolete," but the vision could not be turned into reality. Although the Strategic Defense Initiative, or SDI (which critics dubbed Star Wars, after the science-fiction movie), was given a high priority and billions of dollars for research, the idea of protecting society as a whole from nuclear attack soon appeared hopelessly impractical, given the diverse means of delivering nuclear weapons. The main question became whether SDI could protect key political and military assets from attack, but even here some of the more futuristic ideas—such as using space-based lasers to destroy ballistic missiles just as they were launched—proved technically demanding and expensive. Political support waned.

Meanwhile, Reagan had replaced talks on arms limitation with the Strategic Arms Reduction Talks (START). At first the Soviet Union argued that no progress on strategic arms control was possible so long as SDI was being pursued. Mikhail Gorbachev, who became the Soviet leader in 1985, offered his own vision of how to

U.S. Pres. Ronald Reagan (left) *met with Soviet leader Mikhail Gorbachev at the Reykjavík Summit in October 1986 to discuss the possibility of arms reduction.* David Hume Kennerly/ Getty Images

escape from assured destruction in a speech in January 1986, in which he set out a radical disarmament agenda leading toward a nuclear-free world by the end of the century. In October 1986, at a summit in Reykjavík, Ice., Reagan came close to embracing this vision, although no agreement was reached because he refused Gorbachev's demand to abandon SDI. Nevertheless, the concept of arms reduction had taken hold, and START proceeded with a new emphasis on deep cuts in nuclear arsenals.

The switch to arms reduction suggested that Reagan's critique of MAD had concluded with the view that, given the difficulties of designing and deploying both discriminating offensive options and effective ballistic missile defenses, it was better to do away with nuclear weapons altogether. This constituted a formidable challenge to the orthodox view that nuclear weapons exercised a stabilizing deterrence on international misbehaviour and were a reassurance to allies of the United States, who faced preponderant Soviet conventional forces. Reagan was prevailed upon to moderate his critique, but not before doubts had been created as to the strength of the U.S. commitment to guaranteeing the security of its allies with nuclear weapons.

On the other hand, the alacrity with which Gorbachev embraced complete nuclear disarmament reflected the greater freedom of maneuver available to any Soviet leader as well as the subordinate role of the Warsaw Pact allies. Whereas NATO's European members were eager to lock the United States into their security arrangements for fear that they would be unable to stand alone, the Soviet Union had drawn its allies into a pact that met its own security requirements—that is, extending its form of government into eastern Europe and creating a buffer between it and the hostile capitalist forces of the West. Members of the Warsaw Pact might be beneficiaries of a Soviet nuclear guarantee, but there was no question of shared decision making on nuclear matters. In fact, during the 1970s Soviet doctrine had appeared to have the goal of extracting the maximum regional benefit from its nuclear arsenal—vis-à-vis both western Europe and China—while maintaining Soviet territory as a sanctuary from nuclear devastation. Its priority in any nuclear conflict would have been to confine nuclear exchanges to central Europe while showing a certain respect for U.S. territory as a sanctuary in the hope of reciprocal treatment by the United States. If escalation had appeared inevitable, however, or if the United States had appeared to be preparing a first strike, then Soviet doctrine would have called for a preemptive blow against the United States' long-range arsenal in an effort to reduce damage to the Soviet Union.

This approach was undermined by evidence that U.S. nuclear doctrine and deployment showed no respect for geographic sanctuary and by the Soviets' own recognition of the sheer difficulty of managing a nuclear exchange in such a way as to reduce the vulnerability of Soviet territory. Even before Gorbachev, there had been a discernible trend in military thinking toward emphasizing the opening conventional stage of a war and toward achieving victory within that stage. Gorbachev accelerated this trend. Because he was not prepared to allow overambitious nuclear doctrines to interfere with his objective of improving relations with the West, he was much more prepared than his predecessors to compromise in arms control negotiations. In addition, he was influenced by the April 1986 disaster at the Chernobyl nuclear power plant, which demonstrated that radioactive fallout had little respect for national boundaries.

FLEXIBLE RESPONSE

This gave a new twist to the long-standing debate within NATO over nuclear deterrence. The United States' allies had already learned to live with unavoidable doubts over the quality of the U.S. nuclear guarantee of European security. These began to surface in the 1950s, after the Eisenhower administration had embraced nuclear deterrence and the allies had agreed that it was natural to rely on the most advanced weapons available—especially those in which the United States then enjoyed a clear superiority. The alternative course—relying on conventional forces—would have caused severe economic strains, and there was deep pessimism as to the possibility of ever matching Soviet conventional strength.

The conventional buildup set in motion under the Truman administration had one important requirement: that the Federal Republic of Germany be rearmed. This set in motion a sharp debate in Europe that was coloured by memories of the recent war, but in 1955 a formula was found in which West Germany rearmed but was permitted no chemical or nuclear weapons and was part of NATO's military command. In return, the West German government sought a commitment from its new allies to the concept of forward defense, in which any aggression would be rebuffed at the border between East and West Germany. (With its lack of depth and its concentration of population and industry close to the East, the Federal Republic had no wish for its allies to trade German soil for more time in responding to a Soviet attack.)

Once it had been decided that NATO would not attempt to match Soviet conventional forces, then forward defense meant, in effect, that nuclear deterrence was linked to the inter-German border. European members of NATO had no qualms about this arrangement because it saved them the expense of sustaining large-scale conventional forces, and they did not believe that the Soviet Union had any interest in invading western Europe that would be worth the slightest risk of nuclear war.

In the early 1960s the administration of Pres. John F. Kennedy, which confronted the Soviet Union over the Berlin Wall and the Cuban Missile Crisis, did not take such a relaxed view of Soviet intentions. Given what it saw as the Soviet capacity for retaliation, the

United States thought it unlikely that any president would use nuclear weapons first, and it was hard to see how a credible deterrent could be fashioned out of an incredible nuclear threat. At the very least, the United States insisted, NATO should raise the nuclear threshold—that is, the point at which nuclear weapons would be necessary to stave off conventional defeat. This would be accomplished by extra conventional forces. New analyses suggested that it would be easier than hitherto assumed because previous assessments had exaggerated the strength of the Warsaw Pact. In addition, the Soviet leader, Nikita Khrushchev, who was convinced that nuclear weapons made it unnecessary to maintain vast armies, was imposing major reductions on his generals at that time.

European governments argued in response that conventional forces simply could not provide a sufficient deterrent. Since Soviet territory would not be vulnerable in a conventional war, the Kremlin might judge that the risks of conventional war were acceptable. And even if the Warsaw Pact was defeated, central Europe would still be devastated. Therefore, all war had to be deterred, not just nuclear war.

In 1967 a compromise was found in the doctrine of "flexible response." Under this compromise, the Europeans recognized the U.S. requirement for an extended conventional stage, so that the first shots across the Iron Curtain would not lead automatically to nuclear holocaust, and the United States accepted the need for a clear link between a land war in Europe and its own strategic nuclear arsenal.

CHAPTER 5

NUCLEAR STRATEGY THROUGH THE END OF THE COLD WAR

With the end of the Cold War most of the scenarios of deterrence and war between the superpowers became moot, raising the question of whether there was still a role for nuclear strategy. The answer seemed to lie less in how the old superpowers might use these weapons than in the consequences of their proliferation into a much more complex international system.

LIMITED NUCLEAR WAR

Flexible response did not prescribe a particular course of action; rather, it retained for NATO the possibility that it would be the first to use nuclear weapons and suggested that this initially would involve short-range tactical weapons.

When tactical nuclear weapons such as the Honest John rocket were introduced into the NATO inventory during the 1950s, the U.S. Army had supposed that these could be considered quite separately from intercontinental strategic missiles. If anything, tactical nuclear weapons were closer to conventional weapons and were to be integrated with general-purpose forces. A number of strategic thinkers in the United States, including Henry Kissinger and Robert Osgood, hoped that, if the West could reinforce its military strength in this way, it would be possible to take on communists in limited nuclear wars without resort to incredible threats of massive retaliation.

HENRY KISSINGER

Henry Alfred Kissinger was born on May 27, 1923, in Fürth, Ger. His family immigrated to the United States in 1938 to escape the Nazi persecution of Jews. He became a naturalized citizen in 1943. He served in the U.S. Army during World War II and in the postwar U.S. military government of Germany. After leaving the service, he entered Harvard University, where he received a B.A. (1950) and a Ph.D. (1954). In 1954 he joined the faculty as an instructor, becoming professor of government in 1962 and director of the Defense Studies Program from 1959 to 1969. He also served as a consultant on security matters to various U.S. agencies from 1955 to 1968, spanning the administrations of Dwight D. Eisenhower, John F. Kennedy, and Lyndon B. Johnson.

Henry Kissinger (right) walks with Pres. Richard Nixon in 1972. Kissinger served first as Nixon's national security advisor and later as secretary of state under both Nixon and Gerald Ford. AFP/Getty Images

Kissinger's Nuclear Weapons and Foreign Policy (1957) established him as an authority on U.S. strategic policy. He opposed Secretary of State John Foster Dulles's policy of planning nuclear "massive retaliation" to Soviet attack, advocating instead a "flexible response" combining the use of tactical nuclear weapons and conventional forces, as well as the development of weapons technology in accordance with strategic requirements. That book and The Necessity for Choice (1960), in which Kissinger limited his concept of flexible response to conventional forces and warned of a "missile gap" between the Soviet Union and the United States, had a significant impact on the activities of the Kennedy administration.

Kissinger's reputation as a political scientist led to his role as an adviser to New York governor and Republican presidential aspirant Nelson Rockefeller. In December 1968 Kissinger was appointed by President Nixon as assistant for national security affairs. He eventually came to serve as head of the National Security Council (1969–75) and as secretary of state (September 1973–January 20, 1977).

Kissinger soon emerged as an influential figure in the Nixon administration. His major diplomatic achievements involved China, the Soviet Union, Vietnam, and the Middle East. He developed a policy of warmer U.S. relations with the Soviet Union, détente, which led to the Strategic Arms Limitation Talks (SALT) in 1969. He established the pro-Pakistan policy in the India-Pakistan war of late 1971, helped negotiate the SALT I arms agreement with the Soviet Union (signed 1972), and developed a rapprochement between the United States and the People's Republic of China (1972), the first official U.S. contact with that nation since the Chinese Communists had come to power.

Although he originally advocated a hard-line policy in Vietnam and helped engineer the U.S. bombing of Cambodia (1969–70), Kissinger later played a major role in Nixon's Vietnamization policy—the disengagement of U.S. troops from South Vietnam and their replacement by South Vietnamese forces. On Jan. 23, 1973, after months of negotiations with the North Vietnamese government in Paris, he initialed a cease-fire agreement that both provided for the withdrawal of U.S. troops and outlined the machinery for a permanent peace settlement between the two Vietnams. For this apparent resolution of the Vietnam conflict, Kissinger shared the 1973 Nobel Prize for Peace with the North Vietnamese negotiator, Le Duc Tho (who refused the honour).

After the Arab-Israeli War of 1973, Kissinger used what came to be called shuttle diplomacy in disengaging the opposing armies and promoting a truce between the belligerents. He was responsible for the resumption of diplomatic relations between Egypt and the United States, severed since 1967. He remained in office after Nixon's resignation in 1974, directing the conduct of foreign affairs under President Ford. After leaving office in 1977, Kissinger became an international consultant, writer, and lecturer. In 1983 Pres. Ronald W. Reagan appointed him to head a national commission on Central America. In the 1980s he also served on the President's Foreign Intelligence Advisory Board and the Commission on Integrated Long-Term Strategy. Kissinger's later books include The White House Years (1979) and Does America Need a Foreign Policy?: Toward a Diplomacy for the 21st Century (2001).

However, once the widespread use of battlefield nuclear weapons by NATO was simulated in war games in the 1950s, it became apparent that they would result in such death and destruction that they could in no way be considered conventional. Also, as Warsaw Pact forces obtained comparable capabilities with such weapons as the SS-1 missile, any Western advantage seemed neutralized. Unless a retreating defender used nuclear weapons immediately, any later use could well be over his own territory and against a dispersed enemy. And, if tactical nuclear weapons were used to impose great costs on the enemy, there would be a risk that the conflict could soon escalate to strategic nuclear use. Limited nuclear war, therefore, appeared a contradiction in terms.

European governments were still loath to dispense with the weapons. Although they could not be considered ordinary weapons of war, their close integration with conventional forces meant that they were more likely than U.S. strategic nuclear forces to get entangled in a land war in Europe. The idea was to use the risk of escalating to total nuclear war with the United States as a powerful deterrent effect on the Soviet Union's actions in Europe. According to this strategy, deterrence did not require a certainty that nuclear weapons would be used, only a risk. The consequences of miscalculation were so horrendous that a government dared not gamble. However, the United States, whose own security was now being linked to peace in Europe, was still more concerned that miscalculation might nonetheless take place.

Certainly, NATO's procedures for "going nuclear" were designed to reduce the risk of unauthorized use. But this created a tension between theory, which suggested that deterrence was served by the risk that a conflict might get out of control, and practice, which exhibited a determination not to lose control. The tension was reflected in discussions over how to replace the first generation of tactical nuclear weapons as they became obsolete in the 1970s. If the next generation was made smaller and more precise, then this would imply a readiness to use them to fight a nuclear war rather than simply deter. An apparent readiness to wage nuclear war was at the heart of a controversy over the neutron bomb (actually a thermonuclear missile warhead or artillery shell of enhanced radiation and reduced blast), which was criticized for blurring the boundary between conventional and nuclear weapons and thereby making it much easier to go nuclear.

Even greater controversy was generated by NATO's decision in 1979 to replace the Pershing IA, a medium-range ballistic missile, with two weapons that would constitute a more powerful intermediate-range nuclear force (INF): the Pershing II intermediate-range ballistic missile (IRBM) and the Tomahawk cruise missile. The origins of the program to modernize the INF lay in two western European concerns over the U.S. nuclear guarantee. The first concern resulted from the tendency of the United

A Tomahawk cruise missile, an INF that generated controversy when it was first developed, flies through the air. Time & Life Pictures/Getty Images

States in the Strategic Arms Limitation Talks to concentrate on achieving symmetry between the nuclear forces of the two superpowers while paying little attention to the superiority, within the European theatre, of the Warsaw Pact in both nuclear and conventional weapons. Particularly worrisome was the Soviet SS-20, an IRBM that was first tested in 1974 and deployed in 1977. Although the SS-20 did not signal any shift in Soviet policy (U.S. military bases in Europe and the British, French, and Chinese nuclear forces had long been targeted), it was the first new missile designed for this purpose to have appeared in some time. In 1977 Chancellor Helmut Schmidt of West Germany argued that NATO should not tolerate Soviet superiority in such weapons. This suggested that the imbalance should be dealt with either through arms control or by an equivalent Western effort to upgrade its own INF.

The second concern placed far less stress on the SS-20 and more on the requirements, within NATO's strategy of flexible response, to be able to strike Soviet territory with systems based in western Europe in the event of full-scale war on the Continent. This requirement existed irrespective of the new Soviet missiles, and it was becoming problematic because of the age of NATO's medium bombers and the lack of any U.S. intermediate-range land-based missile in Europe. A modernized INF made more sense than systems designed for battlefield use because they posed a direct threat to the Soviet homeland and thus challenged Soviet ideas of confining any nuclear exchanges to NATO and Warsaw Pact countries, with superpower territory accorded sanctuary status.

However, large-scale protests sprang up in Europe and North America after the decision to modernize. Voicing a concern that a new arms race was getting under way in Europe, they took on special urgency following the Soviet invasion of Afghanistan (two weeks after NATO's decision on the INF), with the decline of arms control, and with the election of Ronald Reagan, who had a hawkish reputation, to the U.S. presidency. The strength of the protests encouraged NATO to moderate its policy. The rationale for modernizing the INF was switched from the requirements of flexible response to the more politically marketable aim of matching the deployment of the SS-20, and in November 1981, at the start of negotiations on this issue, Reagan offered to eliminate NATO's INF if all SS-20s were removed. This "zero option" was rejected by Leonid Brezhnev,

and, despite warnings from the Soviet Union that deployment of a modernized INF would mean the end of negotiations, the first Tomahawk and Pershing II missiles were delivered in late 1983. Yury Andropov promptly broke off the INF talks, hoping to force a breach in the unanimity of the NATO allies, but, when the expected crisis failed to arise, Konstantin Chernenko agreed to resume negotiations. Soon afterward Gorbachev was in charge, and he decided that the zero option was in the Soviet interest: eliminating the INF would remove a direct threat to Soviet territory in return for removing a larger number of Soviet missiles that could strike only the allies of the United States. In December 1987, Gorbachev and Reagan signed the Intermediate-Range Nuclear Forces (INF) Treaty.

Reagan's interest in a nuclear-free world—highlighted by SDI, the Reykjavík summit, and the INF Treaty—encouraged discussion among some Europeans of the possibility of a European defense community that would be less dependent upon the United States. In practice this would require the substitution of a French and British strategic nuclear guarantee for an American one. Britain had always, officially at least, committed its strategic nuclear forces (which since the late 1960s had been SLBMs) to NATO. Britain's rationale for maintaining a national nuclear force involved a combination of the political influence that could be brought to bear on its allies, especially the United States, and a claim to be contributing to the overall deterrent posture.

France, by contrast, had always had a much more nationalistic rationale, but after the 1970s, following the introduction of the Pluton short-range missile, which could land only on German territory, it was obliged to consider the role that its *force de frappe* might have in the defense of its allies. In any event, neither Britain nor France was eager to take over from the United States the broader deterrent role; nor were those who had previously sheltered under the U.S. umbrella interested in a European alternative.

Although the United States' allies saw that the treaty had political benefits in improving East-West relations, some strategists worried that it sounded the death knell for nuclear deterrence. One response by NATO was to see whether it would be possible to build up other nuclear systems by way of compensation, but the difficulty here was that the improved political climate undermined public support for such moves. In West Germany the question of modernizing the short-range Lance missile was coloured by the direct and almost unique threat this weapon posed to German territory. There had always been the strongest official support for the traditional concept of nuclear deterrence in that country, but, with the political climate improving, West German politicians such as Chancellor Helmut Kohl came to argue that yet another nuclear modernization program would send the wrong signals to the East. They were also unhappy at the apparent readiness of the United States and Britain to retain

Germany as a battlefield for short-range nuclear exchanges while securing the removal of intermediate- and long-range systems that threatened their own territories. The Soviet Union possessed large numbers of short-range missiles and had been modernizing them for a decade with such systems as the SS-21, but Gorbachev indicated a readiness to negotiate their complete elimination. British Prime Minister Margaret Thatcher and U.S. Pres. George H.W. Bush insisted that this would be imprudent, and, following their lead, NATO agreed in 1989 to postpone modernizing the Lance in the hope that negotiations on conventional force reductions would reach a satisfactory conclusion and thus reduce the importance of nuclear weapons as a means of compensating for the Warsaw Pact's conventional superiority.

By the end of 1989 the issue seemed completely beside the point. The collapse of European communism by the time that Bush met with Gorbachev just off the coast of Malta in December 1989 meant that the Cold War could be declared over. There was nothing left to deter, while the potential targets for NATO's short-range nuclear missiles were embracing liberal democracy and capitalism.

CONVENTIONAL STRATEGY

Over the 1980s, the main consequence of the developing uncertainties surrounding nuclear deterrence was an increased interest in conventional strategy. For the first two decades of the nuclear age, there had been little interest in this area; given the conviction that any war between the great powers would soon go nuclear, there seemed to be little point in preparing for nonnuclear engagements.

Meanwhile, France and Britain fought a number of colonial wars, with France's struggles in Indochina and Algeria particularly protracted and bitter. During the 1960s the United States became steadily involved in Vietnam, in which a weak pro-Western government in the South faced an insurgency backed by a communist government in the North. After 1965 there was a substantial commitment of all elements of U.S. military power, excluding nuclear weapons but including a bombing campaign against the North.

Partly as a result of these conflicts, interest began to revive in the likely character of a conventional war involving the major powers. In the West this was also a result of the adoption of flexible response, which demanded greater attention to conventional warfare. In the East as well, to some extent because of the shift in NATO doctrine, conventional warfare grew in importance. There was some irony in this. Flexible response reflected NATO's concern over Soviet conventional superiority, yet, under Khrushchev, Soviet forces had been cut back dramatically on the assumption that any future war would go nuclear from the start. After Khrushchev was ousted in 1964, the Soviet Union began a major buildup of conventional forces, and in 1967 military exercises were held that indicated the expectation of a substantial conventional

stage at the start of a future war. Besides the need to remain strong in relation to NATO, by the early 1970s the Soviet buildup reflected concern over a possible threat from China, which had become extremely hostile and was rapidly improving relations with the West. Again, there was irony in this development. China and the Soviet Union had finally split in 1963 over Khrushchev's readiness to deal with the West, over his unwillingness to back the Chinese nuclear program, and over a long-standing border dispute between the two countries. Later, the years of the Cultural Revolution (1966–76) convinced Brezhnev that the Chinese were dangerous and unstable; clashes on the border in 1969 led to hints from Moscow that it might take action against China's fledgling nuclear capability.

In the late 1970s this Warsaw Pact buildup, coupled with Soviet-supported operations in such developing countries as Vietnam, Angola, and Ethiopia, stimulated NATO to improve its capacity to resist an offensive and mobilize quickly. This was based on the fear that, without sufficient warning to get mobilization under way, the strength of Soviet frontline and follow-on forces could overwhelm NATO's thin peacetime lines of defense. Growing doubts over the credibility and durability of nuclear deterrence also increased the importance of improving conventional forces.

Even with increased allocations to defense, NATO governments remained pessimistic about their ability to match Warsaw Pact forces. Although the total military power of NATO was much greater, geography favoured the Warsaw Pact, since reserves from the East could reach the front much more quickly than reserves from the United States, which would have to make a hazardous journey across the Atlantic Ocean. Against this pessimism it was noted that greater numbers were normally assumed to be required by the attacker (a ratio of three to one was often cited, although the critical factor was not the overall ratio but the strength of the offense at the point of attack). Technological advances were said to further favour the defense, in that extremely precise and comparatively simple guided weapons could be used to take on tanks and high-performance aircraft, the central actors in any offensive.

This optimism was questioned by other strategic analysts. They noted that the natural advantage accruing to the defense would do so only if the attacker had to force a way through well-prepared defensive positions rather than simply outflank them. The ability to impose attrition on the enemy would be reduced if the enemy was able to fight a war of maneuver, in which an immobile defense might find itself caught off balance. Moreover, in a war of maneuver, the potential benefits of simple air-defense and antitank systems would soon be qualified by the need to make them mobile, which would put them in need of protection as well.

The proponents of maneuver warfare warned that this was the type favoured by the Warsaw Pact. The Soviet Union preferred the offensive because it would make it possible to defeat the enemy quickly, before the full weight of its power could be brought to bear. Soviet doctrine during the 1970s suggested that a key aspect of this offensive would be the neutralization of NATO's nuclear assets by overrunning key installations, with a possible shift to a regional nuclear offensive when the right moment arrived. By the early 1980s doubts over whether a war would last long enough for the right moment ever to arrive, and whether nuclear exchanges could be limited geographically, encouraged a greater stress by the Soviet military on obtaining a victory in the conventional stage.

The maneuver school eventually encouraged a shift in NATO thinking toward more mobile operations, as well as a greater willingness to contemplate attacks on Warsaw Pact territory in an effort to reduce the momentum of a Pact offensive. In 1982 the United States adopted an approach known as AirLand Battle, which emphasized maneuver and the need to see the battlefield in the round, taking advantage of emerging military technologies to synchronize operations and direct fire with greater accuracy. The strategy of "follow-on forces attack" (FOFA), for example, envisaged the holding of a Pact offensive on the ground while attacking the Pact's follow-on forces in the rear with air strikes. Such aggressive defense was criticized by peace movements as being too provocative. Instead, they proposed nonprovocative strategies based on "defensive defense," which would lack any capability to go on the offensive. These ideas proved difficult to turn into practice, as any sort of mobile force could move forward, and few armies would tolerate being deprived of their capacity to counterattack.

Meanwhile, in the Soviet Union concern over the burden of high defense expenditures, combined with an awareness that the arms buildup of the 1970s had triggered a counterresponse from NATO, encouraged "new thinking" that actually picked up on the ideas of defensive defense. These ideas were received by Soviet military commanders with as little enthusiasm as they were received in the West. Nevertheless, they influenced cuts in Soviet forces, announced by Gorbachev in December 1988, that eliminated some military units of a clearly offensive nature without depriving the Warsaw Pact of its offensive options. However modest in themselves, the cuts raised the prospect of an end to the role of these forces in sustaining the Soviet Union's dominance over eastern Europe.

AFTER THE COLD WAR

The demise of the postwar alliance system and the rapid contraction of the Soviet empire in Europe required a rapid reassessment of strategy. For NATO the traditional calculus was turned upside down. There was no longer a conventionally superior opponent. In all respects NATO was far more powerful than any other group of countries. By the end of 1991 the Soviet Union itself had broken up, with its once formidable armed forces

in some disarray. If there were dangers in Europe, they were soon recognized not as the traditional threats of a rising and radical great power but as the disturbing new threat of chronic weakness, which led to questions about the control of nuclear systems within the former Soviet Union and to the revival of older conflicts and rivalries within Europe that had been suppressed during the Cold War.

Concerned about disorder within the Soviet Union, the United States, instead of worrying about new tactical nuclear weapons or even pausing to design a new arms control framework to deal with the problem, soon took unilateral measures to withdraw some nuclear weapons from land and sea deployments—all in the justified expectation that Russia would reciprocate. The strategic weapons were handled through the START process. In a series of agreements over the following decade, the United States and Russia pledged to shrink their respective stockpiles to about 2,000 warheads by 2012, a reduction of more than 80 percent. At the time of ratification of the last agreement by U.S. Pres. George W. Bush and Russian Pres. Vladimir Putin in 2003, U.S. strategic nuclear forces consisted of some 500 Minuteman III ICBMs, 14 Trident submarines equipped with 24 ballistic missiles, and about 200 bombers. No new strategic systems were under development, although there had been some work done on new nuclear warheads. The Russian force had more than 500 ICBMs, 12 ballistic missile submarines with fewer than 300 missiles, and fewer than 80 aircraft.

The Russian numbers included the SS-27 ICBM, which was still under production.

The slow pace of reductions frustrated disarmament advocates, who supposed that the end of the Cold War had strengthened the case for the complete abolition of nuclear weapons. The U.S. and Russian governments agreed that they were no longer enemies, yet the continued presence of massive arsenals created when they were ideological foes meant that there was an ever-present risk of a terrible accident or unauthorized launch. However, the case for abolition made little headway in NATO countries, although a more modest process of marginalizing of nuclear weapons was accepted. There was now no interest whatsoever in even threatening that a war might "go nuclear," and there was every incentive to keep remaining weapons on a low-alert status to reduce the risks of unauthorized use. Western economic dominance and technological leadership, it was assumed, would deliver the means to defeat all comers in a conventional war. In January–February 1991 this point was made emphatically by Operation Desert Storm, the main engagement in the Persian Gulf War, in which an overwhelmingly superior conventional coalition force led by the United States forced Iraq to abandon Kuwait (occupied the previous August).

The war was conducted along the lines of the AirLand Battle approach against an opponent that boasted a large and well-equipped army but little in the way of air defense. The United States' overwhelming

Russian Pres. Vladimir Putin (left) *walks with U.S. Pres. George W. Bush in Sept. 2003. Earlier that year, both countries had ratified SORT, which would require each party to reduce the number of strategic nuclear warheads by 2012.* Stephen Jaffe/AFP/Getty images

air superiority was directed first against Iraq's military infrastructure and equipment and then against the morale of its forward troops, who could do little more than remain dug in. After Desert Storm there was talk of a "revolution in military affairs," a new order in which precision guidance would be combined with advanced sensors and increasingly sophisticated information and communication technologies to produce an unassailable battlefield advantage.

Meanwhile, those on the less-advantaged side of the technological divide continued to develop counter-strategies for asymmetrical warfare, whereby unconventional means might be used to overcome more technically advanced adversaries. In most cases the easiest route was to follow militia-based guerrilla warfare, playing on American memories of the Vietnam War (1954–75) and the bombings of the U.S. embassy and the U.S. Marine base in Beirut in 1983, which caused the United States to withdraw its peacekeeping force. A hurried departure from Somalia in 1993 and a reluctance to follow its NATO allies into peacekeeping operations in the former Yugoslavia suggested that the United States was averse to taking almost any casualties in conflicts where its most vital interests were not engaged. During the Serbian conflict in Kosovo (1998–99), for example, U.S. Pres. Bill Clinton relied on airpower alone to batter Serbia into ending its offensive against the Kosovars, although help was provided on the ground by the Kosovo Liberation Army. This formula of Western airpower fighting with local, and often quite unsophisticated, allies on the ground was even more in evidence in Afghanistan at the end of 2001 in the U.S. campaign against the al-Qaeda terrorist network and its Taliban hosts following the September 11 attacks against the United States.

These attacks on two icons of American economic and military power, the World Trade Center in New York City and the Pentagon in Washington, D.C., using commercial airliners transformed by hijackers into guided missiles, demonstrated one possible form of asymmetrical warfare. This particular method had not been widely contemplated, but considerable attention had been directed to the possibility of acts of "superterrorism," possibly using nuclear weapons but more likely chemical weapons or biological weapons. Such acts would be extreme versions of the more traditional forms of nuclear deterrence, designed to compensate for conventional inferiority—except that now the logic would be more likely to appeal to potential adversaries of the West. Thus, as the Warsaw Pact disappeared, Russian military leaders concluded that they had to forget past promises never to use nuclear weapons first and revive deterrence as their best option against an ascendant NATO. Would the United States, it was asked, have been so ready to go to war on Kuwait's behalf in 1991 if Iraq's nuclear program had reached maturity—even assuming that the Kuwaitis and Saudis themselves would not have capitulated already to Iraqi demands? For countries such as North Korea and Iran, which claimed to be threatened by American power, nuclear weapons retained their attractions for deterrence purposes; indeed, they heightened the risks of conflict for all Western countries. By the start of the 21st century, North Korea was believed

The "smoking gun" containers for radioactive material that were discovered in a warehouse in Iraq in 1991 after the Persian Gulf War. © IAEA Action Team

to have amassed a small stockpile of weapons, although of uncertain reliability, while Iran was determined to acquire uranium-enrichment capabilities that would enable it to build nuclear devices, though it denied that this was its intention. In both cases, these nuclear programs led to a degree of unwelcome international isolation that in turn led to a search for diplomatic compromises.

Iran and North Korea, together with Iraq, were described by U.S. Pres. George W. Bush in January 2002 in his state of the union address as an "axis of evil." Iraq had caused concern even before the Persian Gulf War, when it was clearly intent on acquiring nuclear weapons. After the war it became apparent that Iraq had made far more progress than previously realized in reaching its goal—this despite the fact that it had ratified the Treaty on the Non-proliferation of Nuclear Weapons, as had North Korea. International controls imposed on Iraq following the Gulf War eliminated its nuclear program, but fears that the program was being reconstituted and might then be used to support terrorists was a central part of the United States' rationale for starting the Iraq War in 2003. After U.S. forces occupied Iraq, it became clear that no serious nuclear capability had been resurrected.

At the same time, countries less likely to get involved in major conflicts demonstrated a readiness to eschew nuclear capabilities. In 1993 South Africa revealed that a small arsenal acquired covertly under the apartheid government had been dismantled, while Ukraine, Belarus, and Kazakhstan agreed to give up the systems inherited from the Soviet Union. Argentina and Brazil also moved away from a nuclear weapons capability.

Nor was all proliferation necessarily about deterring Western countries. The most dangerous development was in fact in South Asia. In May 1998 India and Pakistan, both long assumed to be nuclear powers, confirmed their status by testing nuclear weapons within days of each other. Their intractable dispute over Kashmir continued to bring them close to war. Terrorist attacks by Islamist groups, including one against the Indian Parliament in December 2001, led to a particularly dangerous crisis. India blamed Pakistan for not doing enough to deal with terrorists being staged or supplied from its territory. Nevertheless, in order to avoid a conflict that might escalate to nuclear war, India refrained from taking unilateral military action against terrorist camps across the line of control

in Kashmir or directly in Pakistan. The two sides drew away from the brink, and soon afterward a phase of conflict resolution began between the two countries, demonstrating that nuclear deterrence might still have benign effects.

The example of India and Pakistan tended to support those strategic theorists, such as American Kenneth Waltz, who believed that the presence of nuclear weapons would introduce caution and restraint into all conflicts. Others argued that having them in areas of political instability and with unreliable command-and-control systems led to unacceptable risks of disaster. The United States took the view that so long as other states had nuclear arsenals, or even a capacity to inflict death and destruction on a massive scale by other means, then it was only prudent to maintain a substantial arsenal of its own. Even then the administration of George W. Bush claimed in 2001 that it could not be sure of deterring "rogue states," should they acquire a crude long-range missile capable of delivering lethal warheads to the United States. To guard against this possibility, the United States abandoned the ABM Treaty in order to pursue a limited missile-defense system. Although this move was opposed by Russia, its relationship with the United States was so transformed from the Cold War days that it professed not to be too worried, especially as such a system would not eliminate Russia's own nuclear deterrent. Only in 2007, when plans were announced to deploy a few interceptors in Poland

and the Czech Republic to help protect against an Iranian attack, did Moscow object. It was difficult to see what difference such limited defenses could make against a rogue missile strike, not to mention an arsenal of Russia's size, and so the suspicion was aroused that Russia was using the issue simply to make a larger point about its relations with the West. China's relations with the United States were less sure, as China's nuclear arsenal was small enough that it might not survive a first strike, thus possibly limiting its options in some future crisis over Taiwan. These concerns did not acquire the same momentum as those of Russia, however.

Until 1990 the Cold War had provided a clear strategic context for the development of nuclear weapons and thoughts about their employment. The end of the Cold War did not mean the end of the nuclear age. While the major powers were content to keep their nuclear capabilities at the margins of international affairs, new uncertainties revolved around how lesser powers might exploit this terrifying destructive capability.

CHAPTER 6

BIOLOGICAL WEAPONS

Biological weapons, also called germ weapons, are any of a number of disease-producing agents—such as bacteria, viruses, rickettsiae, fungi, toxins, or other biological agents—that may be utilized as weapons against humans, animals, or plants.

Biological weapons, like chemical weapons and nuclear weapons, are commonly referred to as weapons of mass destruction, although the term is not truly appropriate in the case of biological armaments. Lethal biological weapons may be capable of causing mass deaths, but they are incapable of mass destruction of infrastructure, buildings, or equipment. Nevertheless, because of the indiscriminate nature of these weapons, as well as the potential for starting widespread pandemics, the difficulty of controlling disease effects, and the simple fear that they inspire, most countries have agreed to ban the entire class. A total of 176 countries have signed, and of that number 163 have ratified, the Biological Weapons Convention (BWC), which was opened for signature in 1972. Under the terms of the BWC, member states are prohibited from using biological weapons in warfare and from developing, testing, producing, stockpiling, or deploying them. Nevertheless, a number of states have continued to pursue biological warfare capabilities, seeking a cheaper but still deadly strategic weapon rather than following the more difficult and expensive path to nuclear weapons. In addition, the threat that some deranged individual or terrorist organization will manufacture or steal biological weapons is a growing security concern.

BIOLOGICAL WARFARE AGENTS

Biological warfare agents differ greatly in the type of organism or toxin used in a weapons system, lethality, length of incubation, infectiousness, stability, and ability to be treated with current vaccines and medicines. There are five different categories of biological agents that could be weaponized and used in warfare or terrorism. These include:

- Bacteria—single-cell organisms that cause diseases such as anthrax, brucellosis, tularemia, and plague.
- Rickettsiae—microorganisms that resemble bacteria but differ in that they are intracellular parasites that reproduce inside cells; typhus and Q fever are examples of diseases caused by rickettsia organisms.
- Viruses intracellular parasites, about $1/100$ the size of bacteria, that can be weaponized to cause diseases such as Venezuelan equine encephalitis.
- Fungi—pathogens that can be weaponized for use against crops to cause such diseases as rice blast, cereal rust, wheat smut, and potato blight.
- Toxins—poisons that can be weaponized after extraction from snakes, insects, spiders, marine organisms, plants, bacteria, fungi, and animals; an example of a toxin is ricin, which is derived from the seed of the castor bean.

Some of these biological agents have properties that would make them more likely candidates for weaponization owing to their lethality, ability to incapacitate, contagiousness or noncontagiousness, and hardiness and stability, and other characteristics.

Among the agents deemed likely candidates for biological weapons use are the toxins ricin, staphylococcal enterotoxin B (SEB), botulinum toxin, and T-2 mycotoxin and the infectious agents responsible for anthrax, brucellosis, cholera, pneumonic plague, tularemia, Q fever, smallpox, glanders, Venezuelan equine encephalitis, and viral hemorrhagic fever. In addition, various states at various times have looked into weaponizing dozens of other biological agents.

ANTHRAX

Anthrax is an acute, infectious, febrile disease of animals and humans caused by Bacillus anthracis, *a bacterium that under certain conditions forms highly resistant spores capable of persisting and retaining their virulence for many years. Anthrax most commonly affects grazing animals such as cattle, sheep, goats, horses, and mules, but humans also can develop the disease.*

Anthrax in humans occurs as a cutaneous, pulmonary, or intestinal infection. The most common type, cutaneous anthrax, occurs as a primary localized infection of the skin in the form of a carbuncle. It usually results from handling infected material, lesions occurring mostly on the hands, arms, or neck as a small pimple that develops rapidly into a large vesicle with a black necrotic centre (the malignant pustule). There are also bouts of shivering and chills, but there is little other disability. In more than 90 percent of the cases of anthrax in humans, the bacilli remain within the skin sore. However, the bacilli may escape from the sore and spread via a lymph channel to the nearest lymph node, where their spread is usually halted. Only seldom do the bacilli invade the bloodstream, causing rapidly fatal septicemia (blood poisoning), internal bleeding, and, sometimes, meningitis.

Pulmonary anthrax, called inhalation anthrax (woolsorters' disease), affects principally the lungs and pleura and results from inhaling anthrax spores (e.g., in areas where hair and wool are processed). Inhalation anthrax is occasionally transmitted to humans by spore-contaminated brushes or by wearing apparel such as furs and leather goods. This form of the disease usually runs a rapid course and terminates fatally due to the suffocating pneumonia that results. The intestinal form of the disease, which sometimes follows the consumption of

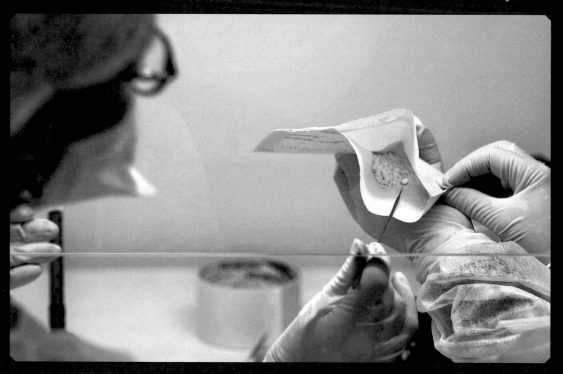

Laboratory technicians examine white powder for anthrax contamination. Mauricio Lima/ AFP/Getty Images

contaminated meat, is characterized by an acute inflammation of the intestinal tract, vomiting, and severe diarrhea.

The bacterium that causes anthrax has a number of attributes that, in combination, make it suitable as a biological weapon. In addition to being widely available—located around the world in soil and in diseased animals and their remains—B. anthracis spores are small enough to lodge readily in the lungs of humans. The anthrax bacterium has a short incubation period and is highly lethal, requiring only a small amount to cause a mass casualty effect. Indeed, aerosolized forms of anthrax sprayed over a large population centre or a massed military force are capable of lethality approaching or exceeding that of a nuclear weapon. Moreover, anthrax can be produced inexpensively, in larger quantities than can other biological warfare agents, and in facilities that are relatively easy to hide. It is more resilient to degradation from ultraviolet light than most other biological agents. Finally, anthrax can be converted into either a powder or a liquid, allowing it to be used in a number of types of weapons systems that utilize a variety of delivery means, including missiles, bombers, artillery, mortars, or crop dusters and similar aircraft.

Anthrax has been weaponized by a number of states. Before it terminated its offensive biological weapons program in 1969, the United States had a significant anthrax weapons program. The former Soviet Union developed the world's largest biological weapons program, which it clandestinely continued 20 years beyond the date when it signed the Biological Weapons Convention of 1972, which prohibited the development and stockpiling of biological weapons. Iraq, under the rule of Saddam Hussein, also developed anthrax and a number of other biological weapons agents but was obliged to destroy such weapons after the Persian Gulf War of 1990–91. At least 14 other nations are believed to have biological weapons programs.

Several effective vaccines have been developed to protect against possible anthrax infection, including Anthrax Vaccine Adsorbed (AVA), the vaccine developed to protect United States military personnel. The anthrax vaccine can provide protection to most recipients, although a small percentage do not acquire complete immunity. However, if vaccinated military personnel were to encounter a massive dose of anthrax, such as might be encountered on a battlefield, even a sensitized immune system could be overwhelmed; a well-fitting mask with fine-grain filters would be necessary to provide protection in such instances.

DEFENSE AGAINST BIOLOGICAL WEAPONS

Because some biological weapons can be produced with relative ease in spite of the presence of an international treaty banning their use, many countries have instituted means for defending their military forces as well as their civilian populations against an attack by hostile forces or terrorists.

MILITARY DEFENSE

Most weaponized lethal biological agents are intended to be delivered as aerosols, which would cause infections when breathed by the targeted personnel. For this reason, the most effective defense against biological weapons is a good protective mask equipped with filters capable of blocking bacteria, viruses, and spores larger than one micron (one micrometre; one-millionth of a metre) in cross section from entry into the wearer's nasal passages and lungs. Protective overgarments, including boots and gloves, are useful for preventing biological agents from contacting open wounds or breaks in the skin. Also, decontaminants can neutralize biological agents in infected areas after a biological attack.

Developing and fielding effective biological weapon sensors that can trigger an alarm would allow personnel to don masks before exposure, get into protective overgarments, and go inside, preferably into toxic-free collective protection shelters. Medical teams could then immediately go into action to check and treat those who may have been exposed.

Biological warfare attacks can be made less effective, or ineffective, if the targeted persons have been vaccinated against the specific disease-causing agent used in an attack.

CIVIL DEFENSE

Civil defense against biological weapons has greatly improved since the Sept. 11, 2001, attacks in the United States, but

progress does not necessarily equal success. A successful civil defense against major biological attacks requires that significant progress be made in sensors, warning systems, vaccines, medicines, training of responders, and public education, as well as in planning of emergency procedures. These aspects of civil defense are described briefly in this section, using as examples certain practices put into effect in the United States since September 11.

The foundation of any civil defense against a biological weapons attack is the medical system that has already been set up to deal with naturally occurring diseases. Special vaccines have been created, tested, and approved to deal with the two most lethal biological agents that can also be most easily weaponized: anthrax and smallpox. For example, the U.S. government has enough smallpox vaccine to vaccinate the entire American population and enough anthrax vaccine to inoculate at least every member of the U.S. military.

Effective vaccines for plague and cholera now exist and have been approved for use, but only small quantities have been produced, far short of what might be needed if large numbers of people were to be infected. Furthermore, in the United States a number of vaccines are still in the Investigational New Drug (IND) category and await further trials before the Federal Drug Administration (FDA) can validate their effectiveness and safety.

Included among these are vaccines for Q fever, tularemia, Venezuelan equine encephalitis, viral hemorrhagic fever, and botulism.

Work continues on finding effective vaccines for preventing infections from glanders, brucellosis, staphylococcal enterotoxin B, ricin, or T-2 mycotoxins—all biological agents that some countries have researched for military use or have weaponized in the past. In some cases where vaccines are not yet available, medicines have been developed that help the sick to recover. In addition, long-term medical research is being conducted to investigate the possibility of developing vaccines and supplements that, when administered, might raise the effectiveness of the recipient's immune system to protect against the whole spectrum of probable biological weapon agents.

One U.S. civil defense program that might make a difference in a biological emergency is the Strategic National Stockpile program, which has created 50-ton "push packages" of vaccines, medicines, decontamination agents, and emergency medical equipment, which are stored in a dozen locations across the country in preparation for emergencies. Furthermore, every U.S. state has bioterrorism response plans in place, including plans or guidelines for mass vaccinations, triage, and quarantines. The U.S. Centers for Disease Control and Prevention (CDC) has also drafted model

legislation on emergency health powers for states to adopt in order to deal with such crises.

A new emergency response system was created in the United States following the September 11 attacks. The National Guard also increased the number of its Weapons of Mass Destruction Civil Support Teams, which respond to chemical, biological, radiological, or nuclear weapons attacks—augmenting the police, fire, and medical first responders in the local area of any attacks. In addition, the Department of Homeland Security, working with the Department of Health and Human Services, invested heavily in passive defenses against biological attacks, focusing on such programs as Project BioShield and the Laboratory Response Network. The CDC also embarked on a training program on bioterrorism for thousands of medical lab technicians, and the National Institutes of Health funded new biocontainment research laboratories to further research in vaccines, medicines, and bioforensics.

Sensors to detect the presence of biological agents in the air, in water, or on surfaces are still relatively ineffective, but the aim of research is to create a "detect-to-warn" system that would provide enough time for potential victims to don masks, cover up, and take shelter before they were infected. The current "detect-to-treat" capability is unsatisfactory, since responders would be treating many persons already infected. Most current biological detectors are point detectors, which are not capable of giving advance warning after scanning an airborne cloud of particles to discern if those particles contain biological agents of a specific type.

BIOLOGICAL WEAPONS IN HISTORY

The direct use of infectious agents and poisons against enemy personnel is an ancient practice in warfare. Indeed, in many conflicts diseases have been responsible for more deaths than all the employed combat arms combined, even when they have not consciously been used as weapons.

PRE-20TH-CENTURY USE OF BIOLOGICAL WEAPONS

One of the first recorded uses of biological warfare occurred in 1347, when Mongol forces are reported to have catapulted plague-infested bodies over the walls into the Black Sea port of Caffa (now Feodosiya, Ukr.), at that time a Genoese trade centre in the Crimean Peninsula. Some historians believe that ships from the besieged city returned to Italy with plague, starting the Black Death pandemic that swept through Europe over the next four years and killed some 25 million people (about one-third of the population).

In 1710 a Russian army fighting Swedish forces barricaded in Reval (now Tallinn, Est.) also hurled plague-infested corpses over the city's walls. In 1763 British troops besieged at Fort Pitt (now Pittsburgh) during Pontiac's Rebellion passed blankets infected with smallpox virus to the Indians, causing a devastating epidemic among their ranks.

BIOLOGICAL WEAPONS IN THE WORLD WARS

During World War I (1914–18), Germany initiated a clandestine program to infect horses and cattle owned by Allied armies on both the Western and Eastern fronts. The infectious agent for glanders was reported to have been used. For example, German agents infiltrated into the United States and surreptitiously infected animals prior to their shipment across the Atlantic in support of Allied forces. In addition, there reportedly was a German attempt in 1915 to spread plague in St. Petersburg in order to weaken Russian resistance.

The horrors of World War I caused most countries to sign the 1925 Geneva Protocol banning the use of biological and chemical weapons in war. Nevertheless, Japan, one of the signatory parties to the protocol, engaged in a massive and clandestine research, development, production, and testing program in biological warfare, and it violated the treaty's ban when it used biological weapons against Allied forces in China between 1937 and 1945. The Japanese not only used biological weapons in China, but they also experimented on and killed more than 3,000 human subjects (including Allied prisoners of war) in tests of biological warfare agents and various biological weapons delivery mechanisms. The Japanese experimented with the infectious agents for bubonic plague, anthrax, typhus, smallpox, yellow fever, tularemia, hepatitis, cholera, gas gangrene, and glanders, among others.

Although there is no documented evidence of any other use of biological weapons in World War II, both sides had active research and development (R&D) programs. The Japanese use of biological warfare agents against the Chinese led to an American decision to undertake biological warfare research in order to understand better how to defend against the threat and provide, if necessary, a retaliatory capability. The United Kingdom, Germany, and the Soviet Union had similar R&D programs during World War II, but only Japan has been proved to have used such weapons in the war.

BIOLOGICAL WEAPONS IN THE COLD WAR

In the Cold War era, which followed World War II, both the Soviet Union and the United States, as well as their respective allies, embarked on large-scale biological warfare R&D and weapons production programs. These programs were required by law to be halted and dismantled upon the signing of the BWC in 1972 and the entry into force of that treaty in 1975. In the case of the United States and its allies, compliance with the terms of the treaty appears to have been complete. Such was not the case with the Soviet Union, which conducted an aggressive clandestine biological warfare program even though it had signed and ratified the treaty. The lack of a verification regime to check members' compliance with the BWC made it easier for the Soviets to flout the treaty without being detected.

After the demise of the Soviet Union in 1991 and its subsequent division into 15 independent states, Russian Pres. Boris Yeltsin confirmed that the Soviet Union had violated the BWC, and he pledged to terminate what remained of the old Soviet biological weapons program. However, another problem remained—that of the potential transfer of information, technical assistance, production equipment, materials, and even finished biological weapons to states and groups outside the borders of the former Soviet Union. The United States and the former Soviet republics pledged to work together to contain the spread of biological warfare capabilities. With financing from the U.S. Cooperative Threat Reduction Program and other sources, help in obtaining civilian jobs in other fields was also made available for some of the estimated 60,000 scientists and technicians who worked in the Soviet biological warfare programs.

YELLOW RAIN

After the communist victories in Southeast Asia in 1975, the new regimes in Vietnam and Laos launched pacification campaigns against Hmong tribes in northern Laos who had assisted the former noncommunist governments and their principal ally, the United States. That summer, refugees began to report that Laotian aircraft were dropping an oily yellow liquid that made a sound like rain when it fell on roofs, roads, or leaves—what the Hmong called "yellow rain." High-dose exposure to this substance reportedly caused symptoms such as bleeding from the nose and gums, tremors, seizures, blindness, and, in some cases, death. Further reports surfaced of similar experiences by Khmer tribes in Cambodia in 1978 and by anti-Soviet resistance fighters in Afghanistan in 1979.

In 1981 the United States accused the Soviet Union of supplying their allies in Laos and Vietnam with trichothecene mycotoxins, a poison produced by fungi that was known to have potential as a biological weapon. Soviet officials denied the charge, and some leading U.S. scientists also questioned the evidence, saying that there were plausible natural causes for the events and symptoms, such as the airborne release of feces by swarms of giant Asian honeybees. Critics also questioned the reliability of the refugees' testimony and the integrity of laboratory analyses conducted on samples of the substance. To this day, the source of the yellow rain is not definitively settled.

BIOLOGICAL WEAPONS PROLIFERATION

Of the more than 190 members of the United Nations, only a dozen or so are strongly suspected of having ongoing biological weapons programs. However, such programs can be easily hidden and disguised as vaccine plants and benign pharmaceutical production centres. Biological weapons are not as expensive to manufacture as nuclear weapons, yet a lethal biological weapon might nonetheless be the strategic weapon that would win a war. This prospect of military advantage might tempt some regimes to acquire the weapons, though perhaps clandestinely.

Since the BWC has no existing verification or inspection procedures to verify compliance by its signatories, cheating on the treaty might be done with no outside proof to the contrary. It is entirely possible that even a small and relatively poor state might successfully embark on a biological warfare program with a small capital investment and a few dozen biologists, all of which could be secretly housed within a few buildings. In fact, a biological weapons program might also be within the technical and financial reach of a terrorist organization. In summary, the degree of biological weapons proliferation is highly uncertain, difficult to detect, and difficult to quantify.

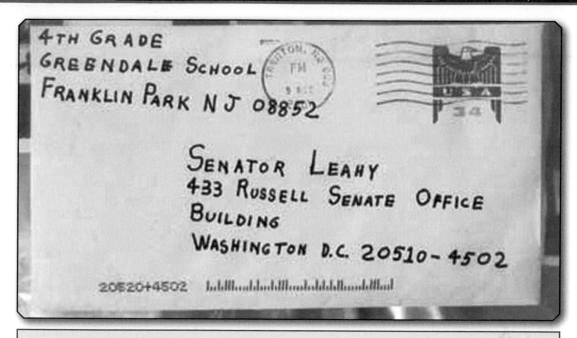

4TH GRADE
GREENDALE SCHOOL
FRANKLIN PARK NJ 08852

SENATOR LEAHY
433 RUSSELL SENATE OFFICE
BUILDING
WASHINGTON D.C. 20510-4502

20520+4502

Anthrax-laden letters, such as this one addressed to Sen. Patrick Leahy of Vermont, were sent to a number of prominent American officials, journalists, and media outlets in the fall of 2001 in an act of biological terrorism. Getty Images

BIOLOGICAL TERRORISM

Biological weapons have been used in a few instances in the past by terrorist organizations. In the 1980s, followers of the exiled Indian self-proclaimed guru Bhagwan Shree Rajneesh settled on a ranch in Wasco county, Oregon. The "Rajneeshies" took political control of the nearby town of Antelope, changing its name to Rajneesh, and in 1984 they attempted to extend their political control throughout the county by suppressing voter turnout in the more populous town of The Dalles. Leading up to the countywide elections, cult members experimented with contaminating groceries, restaurants, and the water supply in The Dalles with *Salmonella* bacteria. Their efforts made at least 751 people ill. The plot was not discovered until the year after the attack, when one of the participants confessed.

In the period from April 1990 to July 1995, the AUM Shinrikyo sect used both biological and chemical weapons on targets in Japan. The members' biological attacks were largely unsuccessful because they never mastered the science and technology of biological warfare; nevertheless, they attempted four attacks using anthrax and six using botulinum toxin on various targets, including a U.S. naval base at Yokosuka.

Al-Qaeda operatives have shown an interest in developing and using biological weapons, and they operated an anthrax laboratory in Afghanistan prior to its being overrun by U.S. and Afghan Northern Alliance forces in 2001–02. In 2001 anthrax-laden letters were sent to many politicians and other prominent individuals in the United States. The letters killed 5 people and sent 22 to the hospital while forcing the evacuation of congressional office buildings, the offices of the governor of New York, several television network headquarters, and a tabloid newspaper office. This event caused many billions of dollars in cleanup, decontamination, and investigation costs. In early 2010, more than eight years after the mailings, the Federal Bureau of Investigation finally closed its investigation, having concluded that the letters had been mailed by a microbiologist who had worked in the U.S. Army's biological defense effort for years and who had committed suicide in 2008 after becoming a suspect in the investigation.

Information on the manufacture of biological and chemical weapons has been disseminated widely on the Internet, and basic scientific information is also within the reach of many researchers at biological laboratories around the world. Unfortunately, it thus seems likely that poisons and disease agents will be used as terrorist weapons in the future.

CHAPTER 7

CHEMICAL WEAPONS

Chemical weapons are chemical compounds, usually toxic agents, that are intended to kill, injure, or incapacitate enemy personnel. Like nuclear weapons and biological weapons, chemical weapons are often classified as weapons of mass destruction. Under the Chemical Weapons Convention (CWC) of 1993, the use of chemical weapons in war is prohibited, as is all development, production, acquisition, stockpiling, and transfer of such weapons.

TYPES OF CHEMICAL WEAPONS

Chemical weapons are chemical agents, whether gaseous, liquid, or solid, that are employed because of their direct toxic effects on humans, animals, and plants. They inflict damage when inhaled, absorbed through the skin, or ingested in food or drink. Chemical agents become weapons when they are placed into artillery shells, land mines, aerial bombs, missile warheads, mortar shells, grenades, spray tanks, or any other means of delivering the agents to designated targets.

Not all poisonous substances are considered suitable for weaponization, or use as chemical weapons. Thousands of such chemical compounds exist, but only a few dozen have been used as chemical warfare agents since 1900. The compounds of most utility must be highly toxic but not too difficult to handle. Furthermore, the chemical must be able to withstand the heat developed when delivered in a bursting shell, bomb, mine, or warhead. Finally, it must be resistant to water and oxygen in the atmosphere in order to be effective when dispersed.

CHEMICAL AGENTS

Since World War I, several types of chemical agents have been developed into weapons. These include choking agents, blister agents, blood agents, nerve agents, incapacitants, riot-control agents, and herbicides.

CHOKING AGENTS

Choking agents were employed first by the German army and later by the Allied forces in World War I. The first massive use of chemical weapons in that conflict came when the Germans released chlorine gas from thousands of cylinders along a 6-km (4-mile) front at Ypres, Belg., on April 22, 1915, creating a wind-borne chemical cloud that opened a major breach in the lines of the unprepared French and Algerian units. The Germans were not prepared to exploit the opening, though, which gave the French and Algerians time to rush reinforcements into the line. Eventually both sides mastered the new techniques of using choking agents such as chlorine, phosgene, diphosgene, chloropicrin, ethyldichlorasine, and perfluoroisoboxylene and launched numerous attacks—though without any militarily significant breakthroughs once each side had introduced the first crude gas masks and other protective measures. Phosgene was responsible for roughly 80 percent of all deaths caused by chemical arms in World War I.

Choking agents are delivered as gas clouds to the target area, where individuals become casualties through inhalation of the vapour. The toxic agent triggers the immune system, causing fluids to build up in the lungs, which can cause death through asphyxiation or oxygen deficiency if the lungs are badly damaged. The effect of the chemical agent, once an individual is exposed to the vapour, may be immediate or can take up to three hours. A good protective gas mask is the best defense against choking agents.

BLISTER AGENTS

Blister agents were also developed and deployed in World War I. The primary form of blister agent used in that conflict was sulfur mustard, popularly known as mustard gas. Casualties were inflicted when personnel were attacked and exposed to blister agents like sulfur mustard or lewisite. Delivered in liquid or vapour form, such weapons burned the skin, eyes, windpipe, and lungs. The physical results, depending on level of exposure, might be immediate or might appear after several hours. Although lethal in high concentrations, blister agents seldom kill. Modern blister agents include sulfur mustard, nitrogen mustard, phosgene oxime, phenyldichlorarsine, and lewisite. Protection against blister agents requires an effective gas mask and protective overgarments.

BLOOD AGENTS

Blood agents, such as hydrogen cyanide or cyanogen chloride, are designed to be delivered to the targeted area in the form of a vapour. When inhaled, these agents prevent the transfer of oxygen to the cells, causing the body to asphyxiate. Such chemicals block the enzyme that is necessary for aerobic metabolism, thereby denying oxygen to the red blood cells, which has an immediate effect similar to that of carbon monoxide. Cyanogen inhibits the proper utilization of oxygen within the blood cells, thereby "starving" and damaging the heart. The best defense against blood agents is an effective gas mask.

NERVE AGENTS

The most lethal and important chemical weapons contain nerve agents, which affect the transmission of impulses through the nervous system. A single drop on the skin or inhaled into the lungs can cause the brain centres controlling respiration to shut down and muscles, including the heart and diaphragm, to become paralyzed. Poisoning by nerve agents causes intense sweating, filling of the bronchial passages with mucus, dimming of vision, uncontrollable vomiting and defecation, convulsions, and finally paralysis and respiratory failure. Death results from asphyxia, generally within a few minutes of respiratory exposure or within hours if exposure was through a liquid nerve agent on the skin. Defense against nerve agents requires a skin-tight gas mask and special protective overgarments.

In the mid-1930s chemists working for the German chemical corporation IG Farben developed the first organophosphorus compound with an extremely high toxicity; this became the nerve agent known as tabun (GA). As much as 12,000 tons was produced for the German army in World War II, although it was never used. Another nerve agent, sarin (GB), was first produced in 1938, and a third, soman (GD), was introduced in 1944; both were also invented in Germany. These three German nerve agents, the G-series (for German) in U.S. nomenclature, were all seized in large quantities by the Allies at the end of World War II. After the war the United States, the Soviet Union, and a number of other states also produced these and other nerve agents as weapons.

VX, the most famous of the so-called V series of persistent nerve agents (and also the deadliest known nerve agent; V is for *venom*), was developed by chemists at a British government facility in 1952. Britain renounced all chemical and biological weapons in 1956 but traded information on the production of VX with the United States in exchange for technical information on the production of thermonuclear bombs. In 1961 the United States began large-scale production of VX. The only other countries believed to have built up VX arsenals were the Soviet Union, France, and Syria. Following the signing of the CWC in 1993, the United States and Russia began the elimination of their chemical weapons stocks, with a goal of finishing the process by 2012; neither country trains its forces with such weapons at present.

Defense against nerve agents requires a skintight mask and effective protective overgarments.

INCAPACITANTS

A good deal of work has been done on chemicals that can incapacitate, disorient, or paralyze opponents. Experiments have been conducted on a number of hallucinogenic drug compounds—for instance, 3-quinuclidinyl benzilate (BZ), LSD (lysergic acid diethylamide), mescaline, and methaqualone—and at one time the U.S. Army fielded BZ weapons. These chemical weapons are designed not to kill; however, even incapacitants can cause permanent injury or loss of life if employed in high dosages or if they cause accidents.

BZ or LSD may attack the nervous system and derange a victim's mental processes, causing, for example, hallucinations or psychotic thinking. Other incapacitants might cause victims to sleep or to be slow to respond.

RIOT-CONTROL AGENTS

Tear gas and vomiting agents have been produced to control riots and unruly crowds. Commonly used tear gases are chloracetophenone (CN), chloropicrin (PS), dibenz (b, f)-1, 4-oxazepine (CR), and o-chlorobenzylidenemalononitrile (CS). CN, the principal component of the aerosol agent Mace, affects chiefly the eyes. PS and CS are stronger irritants that can burn the skin, eyes, and respiratory tract. Such riot-control agents are banned by the CWC if used as "a method of warfare" but are allowed for domestic police enforcement.

Although the United States signed and ratified the CWC, it has reserved the right to use riot-control agents in certain other situations, including counterterrorist and hostage rescue operations, noncombatant rescue operations outside war zones, peacekeeping operations where the receiving state has authorized the use of force, and military operations against nonstate actors initiating armed conflict.

HERBICIDES

Herbicides are not banned by the CWC unless they are used as "a method of warfare." However, not all state parties to the CWC consider herbicides to be chemical weapons, and these states, therefore, do not recognize their use to be banned by the treaty.

States can attach reservations if they do not directly undermine the essential purposes of the treaty. In this case, the regulation of nonlethal herbicides is less essential than the more dangerous CW agents.

Herbicides can be used to destroy enemy crops and foliage cover. For example, Agent Orange was used extensively by U.S. forces between 1962 and

1971, during the Vietnam War, as a defoliant to deny cover in the jungle to the Viet Cong and to North Vietnamese forces. Other herbicides, such as paraquat, Agent White (picloram and 2,4-D), and Agent Blue (dimethyl arsenic acid), have also been produced to act as chemical weapons.

AGENT ORANGE

Agent Orange was a mixture of herbicides that U.S. military forces sprayed in Vietnam from 1962 to 1971 during the Vietnam War for the dual purpose of defoliating forest areas that might conceal Viet Cong and North Vietnamese forces and destroying crops that might feed the enemy. The defoliant, sprayed from low-flying aircraft, consisted of approximately equal amounts of the unpurified butyl esters of 2,4-dichlorophenoxyacetic acid (2,4-D) and 2,4,5-trichlorophenoxyacetic acid (2,4,5-T). Agent Orange also contained small, variable proportions of 2,3,7,8-tetrachlorodibenzo-p-dioxin—commonly called "dioxin"—which is a by-product of the manufacture of 2,4,5-T and is toxic even in minute quantities. About 50 million litres (13 million gallons) of Agent Orange—containing about 170 kg (375 pounds) of dioxin—were dropped on Vietnam. Agent Orange was one of several herbicides used in Vietnam, the others including Agents White, Purple, Blue, Pink, and Green. The names derived from colour-coded bands painted around storage drums holding the herbicides.

Among the Vietnamese, exposure to Agent Orange is considered to be the cause of an abnormally high incidence of miscarriages, skin diseases, cancers, birth defects, and congenital malformations (often extreme and grotesque) dating from the 1970s.

Many U.S., Australian, and New Zealand servicemen who suffered long exposure to Agent Orange in Vietnam later developed a number of cancers and other health disorders. Despite the difficulty of establishing conclusive proof that their claims were valid, U.S. veterans brought a class-action lawsuit against seven herbicide makers that produced Agent Orange for the U.S. military. The suit was settled out of court with the establishment of a $180,000,000 fund to compensate some 250,000 claimants and their families. Separately, the U.S. Department of Veterans Affairs awarded compensation to about 1,800 veterans.

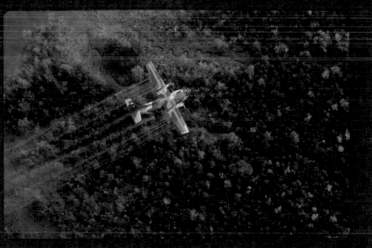

A U.S. Air Force plane sprays Agent Orange over an area of dense foliage in Vietnam. Dick Swanson/Time & Life Pictures/Getty Images

PROPERTIES OF CHEMICAL WEAPONS

Chemical weapons can be categorized by their physical characteristics, such as lethality, persistency, mode of action on the human body, and physical state (i.e., gas, liquid, or solid) when being delivered.

Some chemical agents are highly lethal. For example, nerve agents such as sarin, tabun, soman, and VX can kill almost instantly; a few droplets absorbed through the skin can paralyze and cause death in minutes. At the other end of the lethality spectrum are chemical agents, such as tear gas, that only act as irritants or incapacitants and are unlikely to kill unless used in very large quantities.

Chemical agents also have varied levels of persistency. Some evaporate in minutes or hours and lose their effect rapidly. For example, sarin is a lethal but nonpersistent nerve agent. By contrast, VX can persist for days or weeks in lethal form. This difference in persistency may lead to a different strategic or tactical use of each agent in wartime. A military force may use persistent chemical weapons, such as VX or mustard, to neutralize an air base, seaport, or key staging area for an extended period in order to deny its use to the adversary. On the other hand, nonpersistent chemical weapons, such as sarin, more likely would be employed where only a temporary effect was sought. For example, nonpersistent chemical weapons could be used to breach an enemy line at a point that one's own forces might want to pass through or occupy after the effects had dissipated.

Some poison gases, such as chlorine and hydrogen cyanide, enter the victim's lungs during inhalation. On the other hand, nerve agent droplets might enter through the skin into the bloodstream and nervous system. Still other chemicals can be mixed with food in order to poison enemy personnel when they take their meals.

Finally, chemical weapons might be delivered as aerosols, mortars, artillery shells, missile warheads, mines, or aerial bombs. Most of these have all the ingredients premixed, but newer chemical arms may be so-called binary weapons in which the ingredients are mixed in flight while the weapon is being delivered. Binary weapons are safer and easier to store and handle than more traditional chemical arms.

DEFENSE AGAINST CHEMICAL WEAPONS

While the aim of the CWC is complete elimination of most types of chemical weapons, not all countries have abandoned their chemical warfare capabilities. In particular, some weaker states have pursued chemical weapons programs as deterrents to being attacked by enemies that have either stronger conventional forces or their own weapons of mass destruction, and some regimes have used chemical weapons to threaten especially vulnerable foes outside and even within their own borders. Furthermore, some individuals and militant organizations have acquired or have sought to acquire chemical weapons in order to attack their enemies or to secure their own ends through terror. The continued threat from chemical weapons has led many states to prepare defenses against them and to exert diplomatic pressure on dissenting or noncompliant states to abide by the CWC.

ON THE BATTLEFIELD

Since World War I the military organizations of all the great powers have acquired defensive equipment to cope with emerging offensive chemical weapons. The first and most important line of defense against chemical agents is the individual protection provided by gas masks and protective clothing and the collective protection of combat vehicles and mobile or fixed shelters. Filters for masks and shelters contain specially treated activated charcoal, to remove vapours, and paper membranes or other materials, to remove particles. Such filters typically can reduce the concentration of chemical agents by a factor of at least 100,000. Masks can be donned in less than 10 seconds and can be worn for long periods, even in sleep. Modern protective overgarments are made of fabric containing activated charcoal or other adsorptive forms of carbon. A complete suit typically weighs about 2 kg (4.4 pounds). The fabric can breathe and pass water vapour perspiration. In warm weather, periods of heavy exertion in full protective gear would have to

be limited in order to avoid heat stress. Also, removing such gear in a contaminated environment would raise the risk of becoming a casualty or fatality, and so gear must be removed within toxic-free shelters after following decontamination procedures at the shelter entrance.

Chemical detectors have been developed to help identify levels and places of contamination. These include chemically treated litmus paper used to determine the presence of chemical agents. Other sensors may include handheld assays, vehicles equipped with scoops and laboratory analysis tools, and both point and standoff sensors. Automatic field alarm systems are employed by some military forces to alert personnel to the presence of chemical agents.

Well-equipped troops are supplied with hypodermic needles filled with antidotes to be administered in the event of toxic poisoning from nerve agents. For example, atropine shots can be injected to fight the effects of nerve gas exposures, and different medicines are available to treat casualties.

A number of methods have been found useful in decontaminating areas and people covered with chemical agents, including spraying with supertropical bleach (chlorinated lime) or washing contaminated surfaces or garments with warm soapy water. The challenge is finding and using a decontamination solution that is strong enough to neutralize the chemical agent without damaging the equipment or harming the personnel. In some military forces, modular field hospitals have been developed that are stocked with resuscitation devices for respiratory support and other necessary equipment, decontamination solutions, and staff trained to decontaminate chemical warfare casualties. Collective protective shelters, complete with filters for airflow systems, have been provided to shield personnel in an otherwise contaminated area. Such shelters can provide a toxic-free area for personnel to change clothes, get medical attention, sleep, and take care of bodily functions with less danger of exposure to lethal chemicals.

Chemical agents used against unprotected forces can cause high casualties, fear, and confusion. Thus, personnel facing adversaries equipped with chemical weapons must be trained to don individual protective equipment, seek cover in collective protection shelters, avoid contaminated areas, and rapidly decontaminate personnel and equipment that have been exposed. However, such measures, while necessary to protect against chemical attacks, may expose protected forces to greater casualties from conventional weapons fire and lead to a loss of conventional combat effectiveness. Indeed, exercises have shown that conventional combat effectiveness can be decreased by 25 percent or more for military forces compelled to operate in masks, protective overgarments, special gloves, and boots. This is especially true if temperatures are high and forces are required to stay sealed in their gear for many hours or days without relief. Prolonged wearing of individual

protective equipment can lead to stress, fatigue, disorientation, confusion, frustration, and irritability. Also, heat can build up and lead to dehydration. Thus, there is generally a trade-off between protecting one's force through chemical-protection gear and maintaining conventional fighting effectiveness.

IN CIVILIAN DEFENSE

While most military forces have at least some defense against chemical attack, this is not the case for most civilian populations, which typically have no individual protective equipment (masks, overgarments, boots, or gloves) or collective protection shelters. One notable exception is Israel, which has been at war numerous times since its independence in 1948. Israeli citizens are assigned their own gas masks, and new buildings in Israel must contain a reinforced shelter. Israel also conducts civil defense exercises on a regular basis in order to prepare its citizens for attack.

A further problem for almost every country is the presence in most urban centres of storage or manufacturing facilities that contain toxic industrial chemicals and other toxic materials. A conventional attack on such a site would be the functional equivalent of a chemical weapons attack. Most countries do not have adequate security around such areas.

One response to the threat of a chemical weapons attack on civilian society has been the creation of active, well-trained emergency response teams that know how to identify chemical agents, decontaminate areas and people exposed to chemical weapons, and coordinate rescue operations. Cognizant of the growing risk posed by WMD, the United States in 1998 authorized the creation of 10 National Guard WMD Civil Support Teams (WMD-CST) within its territory; each team was organized, trained, and equipped to handle chemical emergencies in support of local police, firefighters, medical personnel, and other first responders. In subsequent years, dozens of new WMD-CST were authorized, with plans for eventually certifying units for every state and some U.S. protectorates. In addition, the U.S. Centers for Disease Control and Prevention maintains the Strategic National Stockpile, which contains medical supplies and equipment positioned around the country to provide medical help in emergencies, including a chemical weapons attack.

CHEMICAL WEAPONS IN HISTORY

In modern warfare, chemical weapons were first used in World War I (1914–18), during which gas warfare inflicted more than one million of the casualties suffered by combatants in that conflict and killed more than 90,000. In the years since then, chemical arms have been employed numerous times, most notably in the Iran-Iraq War (1980–88). The United States and the Soviet Union, during their decades of confrontation in the Cold War (1945–91), built up enormous stockpiles of chemical weapons. The end of the Cold War enabled these former adversaries to agree to ban all chemical weapons of the types that were developed during World War I (first generation), World War II (second generation), and the Cold War (third generation).

ANTIQUITY

The use of chemical weapons dates back to antiquity, when warring forces frequently poisoned the water supplies of their adversaries. For example, the Athenians poisoned the wells of their rivals as early as 600 bce, and the Spartans, their chief antagonists, in turn hurled burning sulfur pitch over the walls of Athens in 423 bce. In 673 ce the Byzantines defended Constantinople from the Saracen navy by igniting chemicals (known as Greek fire) floating in the sea. During the Middle Ages, Genghis Khan's Mongolian forces employed chemical warfare when they catapulted burning pitch and sulfur into cities they besieged.

AS WEAPONS OF MASS DESTRUCTION

Chemical weapons did not become true WMD until they were introduced in their modern form in World War I (1914–18). The German army initiated modern chemical warfare by launching a chlorine attack at Ypres, Belg., on April 22, 1915, killing 5,000 French and Algerian troops and momentarily breaching their

U.S. soldiers using gas equipment and receiving telephone instructions during the Meuse-Argonne offensive, Varennes-en-Argonne, France, 1918. Encyclopædia Britannica, Inc.

lines of defense. German use of gas and mustard was soon countered by similar tactics from the Allies. By war's end, both sides had used massive quantities of chemical weapons, causing an estimated 1,300,000 casualties, including 91,000 fatalities. The Russian army suffered about 500,000 of these casualties, and the British had 180,000 wounded or killed by chemical arms. One-third of all U.S. casualties in World War I were from mustard and other chemical gases, roughly the ratio for all participants combined. By the war's end, all the great powers involved had developed not only offensive chemical arms but also crude gas masks and protective overgarments to defend themselves against chemical weapon attacks. Altogether, the warring states employed more than two dozen different chemical agents during World War I, including mustard gas, which caused perhaps as many as 90 percent of all chemical casualties (though very few of these casualties were fatal) from that conflict.

Other choking gas agents used included chlorine, phosgene, diphosgene, and chloropicrin. The blood agents included hydrogen cyanide, cyanogen, chlorine, and cyanogen bromide. Arsenic-laced sneeze agents were also used, as were tear gases like ethyl bromoacetate, bromoacetone, and bromobenzyl cyanide.

The horrific casualties of World War I helped persuade many world leaders of the need to ban the use of chemical weapons. A number of proposals were made during the 1920s, and at the 1925 Geneva Conference for the Supervision of the International Traffic in Arms a protocol was approved and signed by most of the world's states. The 1925 Geneva Protocol made it illegal to employ chemical or biological weapons, though the ban extended only to those who signed the treaty. The Geneva Protocol did not ban the production, acquisition, stockpiling, or transfer of such arms, and, critically, it did not contain any verification procedure to ensure compliance.

Despite the popular reaction against this form of warfare and the international agreement banning the use of chemical weapons, chemical arms were used a number of times in the years between the two World Wars. For example, chemical weapons were employed by British forces in the Russian Civil War (1919), Spanish forces in Morocco (1923–26), Italian forces in Libya (1930), Soviet troops in Xinjiang (1934), and Italian forces in Ethiopia (1935–40).

During the Sino-Japanese War (1937–45), Japanese forces employed riot-control agents, phosgene, hydrogen cyanide, lewisite, and mustard agents extensively against Chinese targets. There is no record of chemical warfare among World War II belligerents other than that of the Japanese. The Axis forces in Europe and the Allied forces adopted no-first-use policies, though each side was ready to respond in kind if the other acted first. Indeed, all the major powers developed extensive chemical warfare capabilities as a deterrent to their use.

After World War II, chemical weapons were employed on a number of occasions. Egyptian military forces, participating in Yemen's civil war between royalists and republicans, used chemical weapons, such as nerve and mustard agents, in 1963, 1965, and 1967. During the Soviet intervention into the Afghan War (1978–92), chemical arms, such as mustard and incapacitating agents, were used against the mujahideen rebels. In 1987 Libya used mustard munitions against rebels in Chad. The most extensive post-World War II use of chemical weapons occurred during the Iran-Iraq War (1980–88), in which Iraq used the nerve agents sarin and tabun, as well as riot-control agents and blister agents like sulfur mustard, resulting in tens of thousands of Iranian casualties. Chemical weapons enabled Iraq to avoid defeat, though not obtain victory, against the more numerous Iranian forces. In response to Iraq's use of chemical weapons, Iran made efforts to develop chemical weapons and may have used them against Iraq, a contention that Iran has denied. Furthermore, Iran claims to have ended its program when it signed (1993) and ratified (1997) the CWC. Iraq also used chemical weapons (thought to be hydrogen cyanide, sarin, or sulfur mustard gas) against Iraqi Kurds who were considered unfriendly to the regime of Saddam Hussein. The most notorious such attack was the killing of 5,000 Kurds, including many civilians, in the city of Halabjah in 1988.

BANNING CHEMICAL WEAPONS

During World War I, Germany, France, the United Kingdom, and Russia developed a wide array of chemical arms, including choking, blister, blood, and irritant agents. During World War II, Germany developed nerve agents such as toman, soman, and sarin. After World War II, the British invented VX, a more persistent nerve agent that eventually was deployed by the United States and the Soviet Union.

The World War I chemical agents are referred to as first-generation weapons; the World War II nerve agents are called second-generation weapons; and Cold War chemical agents (such as VX) are known as third-generation weapons. Part of the U.S. arsenal during the Cold War also included CS, a riot-control agent, and BZ, an incapacitant, as well as sarin and VX. The Soviet Union also had a complete chemical weapons arsenal, including "classic" agents from the first, second, and third generation, all of which are now banned by the CWC.

According to some interpretations, the CWC does not cover fourth-generation chemical weapons, so-called nontraditional agents (NTAs), such as some of the binary nerve agents known as "novichoks." There is evidence that Russia inherited NTAs from the former Soviet arsenals.

Negotiations to secure a multilateral chemical disarmament treaty began in the early 1960s at the United Nations. Issues that separated the sides were the kinds of verification procedures for checking on treaty compliance, whether all or part of the weapons stocks should be dismantled, and the sanctions to be levied against violators. Real progress did not take place until the period 1986–91, when relations between the Soviet Union and the United States improved after the rise to power of Soviet leader Mikhail Gorbachev. With the dissolution first of the Warsaw Pact in 1989 and then of the Soviet Union itself in 1991, a real convergence of political and diplomatic views was made possible. In 1990 bilateral reductions and limits were negotiated in which each state agreed to a limit of 5,000 tons of chemical agents in its chemical weapons arsenal. By 1993 the former enemies were finally willing to agree to a robust on-site verification regime featuring challenge inspections of undeclared sites, a total ban on chemical weapons, and a total dismantling of their stockpiles.

The United Nations Conference on Disarmament adopted the Chemical

Weapons Convention (CWC) on Sept. 3, 1992, and the treaty was opened to signature by all states on Jan. 13, 1993. The CWC entered into force on April 29, 1997, 180 days after the deposit of the 65th instrument of ratification (such as passage by a national assembly).

At the time that the United States and Russia signed the CWC, Russia declared 40,000 metric tons of chemical weapon agents and the United States 30,000 metric tons—stockpiles that dwarfed the combined arsenals of the rest of the world. All were to be destroyed, according to CWC guidelines, by the year 2012, but after several years of work the United States declared it would not be able to finish the job until 2021, and Russia announced that its effort would take until at least 2015. In the early 1990s the U.S. Cooperative Threat Reduction Program was launched to help the states of the former Soviet Union demilitarize their chemical, biological, and nuclear facilities and arsenals and also employ the scientists and technicians from those programs in other, more productive peacetime activities.

All other signatories to the CWC reportedly eliminated their stockpiles, though some states subsequently declared stockpiles that they had previously denied existed. Libya is a case in point. In 2004 Libya decided to part with its chemical and nuclear weapons programs and invited the United States and the United Kingdom to help it dismantle both. Significant progress was made in destroying mustard gas and precursors to other chemical weapons before the country was paralyzed by civil strife in 2011.

United Nations inspection teams entered Iraq after the Persian Gulf War ended in early 1991. Some 40,000 Iraqi chemical weapons were then found and destroyed, and a bunker containing thousands of possibly war-damaged weapons was sealed. After the U.S. invasion of Iraq in 2003, no major stockpile of chemical weapons or dedicated facilities for their manufacture were found in Iraq, contrary to the United States' contention before the invasion. A very few chemical rounds were found among arms storage sites in Iraq, but they were thought to be left over from the Iran-Iraq War. Upon becoming a signatory to the CWC in 2009, Iraq acknowledged its obligation to dispose of its remaining damaged weapons—a complicated and dangerous effort that would take years to complete.

PROLIFERATION AND DETECTION OF CHEMICAL WEAPONS PROGRAMS

The CWC has resulted in the elimination of huge stocks of chemical weapons once held by the principal adversaries of the Cold War. Nevertheless, intelligence services of various countries have reported an increase in the number of states with active chemical weapons programs. When the CWC went into effect in 1997, some 20 countries were reportedly working on chemical weapons, as opposed to only five states in the 1960s. This proliferation of technology and know-how has made it critically important to ensure compliance with treaty obligations and to detect weapons programs at their earliest stages.

CHEMICAL WEAPONS PROLIFERATION

Regimes seek to acquire chemical weapons for a number of reasons. First, they may decide that having such lethal weapons will allow them to "level the playing field" against an adversary with a stronger conventional military force. Second, they may wish to deter attacks by rivals, holding them at bay with the threat of a chemical weapons strike in retaliation. Having one type of weapon of mass destruction might deter the use of the same or another type by a rival. Third, chemical weapons, like other mass casualty weapons such as nuclear and biological arms, may be designed for regime survival in the event that a country is losing a conventional conflict. In this case, possession of chemical warfare capabilities might provide endgame bargaining leverage to establish better terms. For example, in the Iran-Iraq War, Iraq's use of Scud ballistic missiles (with the potential to deliver chemical warheads) against Iranian cities caused major panic in those metropolitan centres and helped persuade the Iranian government to agree to a cease-fire sought by Iraq. Fourth, chemicals can be used as terror weapons to lower enemy morale and weaken support for the rival's war effort. Finally, chemical weapons can be used against unprotected rebellious groups inside a country, as Saddam Hussein illustrated in his chemical weapon strikes against the Kurdish city of Halabjah.

DETECTION OF CLANDESTINE PROGRAMS

Although most states have joined the CWC, some member states may still cheat and deploy a clandestine chemical weapons program. Inspectors from the Organisation for the Prohibition of Chemical Weapons (OPCW; the body that administers the CWC) number only in the hundreds, whereas the estimated number of chemical plants that might be inspected exceed many thousands. Therefore, only a small fraction of sites can be inspected every year. Still other states refuse to ratify the various nuclear, biological, and chemical nonproliferation pacts until their rivals eliminate their own (undeclared) arsenals and join the respective arms-control treaty regimes.

This leads to the question of how a clandestine chemical weapons program can be detected and measured. Using technical means, human intelligence, and on-site inspections, chemical weapons program signatures can be monitored when searching for a hidden cache of weapons or a production process. These signatures include purchases of unique combinations of chemical precursors and equipment, the presence of equipment for chemical weaponization, and the presence of chemical warfare defensive gear in military units. Other signatures are the discovery of trace amounts of chemical warfare agents or chemical weapons degradation products at a production site or in a plant's waste products. Finally, signatures may be the presence of storage bunkers, related manufacturing facilities needed for chemical weaponization, or even the presence of a chemical plant with abnormal input-output flows of materials. Nevertheless, detection of clandestine chemical weapons, banned by the CWC or otherwise, is a difficult challenge, since chemical weapons production can be embedded in commercial chemical production plants and evidence can be eliminated in a short period prior to permitting inspectors onto a site—if they are allowed on at all.

The Australia Group is a standing diplomatic conference made up of representatives from states dedicated to restraining the proliferation of key materials and technologies that could be used to produce chemical or biological weapons. Since its formation in 1985, members of the organization have exchanged information and cooperated with one another to control such exports to suspect buyers. The Australia Group is a strictly voluntary and informal export control regime with no formal guidelines, charter, or constitution.

CHEMICAL WEAPONS AND TERRORISM

Until the 1990s, terrorists had rarely possessed or employed chemical weapons.

However, several states that have sponsored terrorism have also possessed chemical weapons—Libya, Iran, and Iraq—and there is a concern that such countries and groups they sponsor might use chemical weapons in the future.

An example of an organization that learned to produce and use chemical weapons is the AUM Shinrikyo sect in Japan, members of which used sarin nerve agent to kill 12 people and injure more than 1,000 in a March 1995 chemical weapons attack inside the Tokyo subway system. Members of this same group had killed 7 and injured more than 300 in a June 1994 attack in Matsumoto, Japan. They also assassinated one opponent using VX nerve agent in Osaka and injured another by the same means in Tokyo in early 1995. Finally, in May and July 1995, members of the AUM Shinrikyo used hydrogen cyanide in two follow-up strikes in the Tokyo subway that injured four persons. Altogether, the several attacks with three different types of chemical weapons killed 20 people, injured some 1,300, and sent more than 5,600 to the hospital for examination. Casualties would likely have been much higher had the Japanese police not intervened when they did.

Al-Qaeda leaders have shown an interest in acquiring and employing chemical weapons, as indicated by experiments testing the use of hydrogen cyanide on animals in al-Qaeda camps in Afghanistan prior to the September 11 attacks on the United States in 2001.

In addition to other documents showing ongoing research on chemical weapons, al-Qaeda planned and then aborted a chemical attack on the New York City subway system in 2005. Furthermore, al-Qaeda in Mesopotamia (also known as al-Qaeda in Iraq) initiated chlorine attacks in Iraq in 2007. It is believed by some Western analysts that al-Qaeda leaders would not hesitate to use any chemical, biological, radiological, or nuclear weapons that they might acquire. For example, al-Qaeda in Mesopotamia openly issued a public invitation for Muslim chemists, biologists, and physicists to join their cause.

Unfortunately, a substantial amount of information on how to manufacture chemical weapons already exists in the public domain, particularly on the Internet, which is within reach of individuals and groups worldwide.

CHAPTER 8

ARMS CONTROL AND DISARMAMENT

International efforts to reduce or at least limit the development and deployment of armaments have become an urgent and complicated issue since the rapid development of nuclear weapons after 1945 and since the proliferation of biological- and chemical-weapons technology toward the end of the 20th century. Before the rise of weapons of mass destruction, arms-control and disarmament advocates used to contend that armaments races were economically inexpedient and led inevitably to war. In the age of mass destruction, this argument of expedience has been replaced by the argument that the presence of weapons of mass destruction by definition threatens the continued existence of civilization itself. The very concept of arms control implies that generally competitive or antagonistic states should collaborate in certain areas of military policy in order to diminish the likelihood that nuclear, biological, or chemical war would destroy them all.

In a broad sense, arms control grows out of historical state practice in disarmament, which has had, since the 20th century, a long record of successes and failures. A narrower definition of each term, however, reveals key differences between disarmament and arms control. Complete or general disarmament may involve the elimination of a country's entire military capacity. Partial disarmament may consist of the elimination of certain types or classes of weapons or a general reduction (but not elimination) of all classes of weapons. Whereas disarmament agreements usually directly prohibit the possession or production of weapons, arms-control agreements often proceed by setting limitations on the testing, deployment, or use of certain types of weapons. Arms-control advocates generally take a more or less realistic approach to international relations, eschewing pacifism in a world they view as anarchic and as lacking any central authority for settling conflicts. Furthermore, whereas the objective of disarmament agreements is the reduction or elimination of weapons, arms-control agreements aim to encourage countries to manage their weapons in limited cooperation with each other. Disarmament conferences with a large number of participants have often degenerated into public spectacles with shouting matches between the delegations of countries that have resulted in increased tensions. Nevertheless, arms-control efforts, particularly those between the United States and the Soviet Union during the Cold War, proved useful in limiting the nuclear arms race, and, by the end of the 20th century, the term *arms control* was often used to denote any disarmament or arms-limitation agreement.

EARLY EFFORTS

The first international assembly that addressed the issue of arms control (among other issues) was the first Hague Convention (1899). Although this and later Hague conferences failed to limit armaments, they did adopt a number of agreements on territorial and functional matters. Other Hague conferences addressed issues of arbitration and principles and treaties of warfare. The Hague Convention approved prohibitions on the use of asphyxiating gases and expanding bullets (dumdums) and discharges of projectiles or explosives from balloons, though none of these agreements was observed during World War I. After the war, the Washington Conference (1921–22)—before adjourning early—reached disarmament, arms-limitation, and arms-control agreements aimed at halting the naval arms race between the world's leading powers. The United States, the United Kingdom, France, Italy, and Japan agreed to limit the number and tonnage of their capital ships and to scrap certain other ships. At the London Naval Conference (1930), however, Italy and France refused to agree to an extension of the agreement, and Japan withdrew in 1935. In 1925 the Geneva Protocol, which now has some 130 parties, prohibited the use of asphyxiating and poisonous gases and bacteriological weapons in international conflicts, though it did not apply to internal or civil wars. Because many countries retained the right to use such weapons in a retaliatory strike, the Geneva Protocol came to be seen as a broader and more effective agreement that included prohibitions of using such weapons in a first strike.

ARMS-CONTROL AGREEMENTS DURING THE COLD WAR

World War II, during which some 40 to 50 million people died, was by far the bloodiest conflict in human history. The conclusion of the Pacific phase of the war ushered in the atomic age as the United States dropped atomic bombs on the Japanese cities of Hiroshima and Nagasaki in 1945. Two of the victor states, the United States and the Soviet Union, soon began to develop large arsenals of nuclear weapons. The possibility of the mutual destruction of each country by the other in an intercontinental exchange of nuclear-armed missiles prompted them to undertake increasingly serious negotiations to limit first the testing, then the deployment, and finally the possession of these weapons. As precursors, the International Atomic Energy Agency (IAEA) was established in 1957 as an autonomous intergovernmental body, under the auspices of the United Nations, to promote peaceful uses of nuclear technology and to prevent the use of such technology for military purposes; and in 1959 the Antarctic Treaty, signed by 12 countries, including the United States and the Soviet Union, internationalized and demilitarized Antarctica and paved the way for future arms-control agreements between the Soviet Union and the United States. Many of the arms-control agreements of the Cold War period focused on mutual deterrence, a strategy in which the threat of reprisal would effectively preclude an initial attack.

U.S. Presidents Dwight D. Eisenhower and John F. Kennedy considered treaties that sought to control the production of weapons in an attempt to avoid a nuclear conflict. (Kennedy, in particular, was concerned with nuclear proliferation by the People's Republic of China.) During the Cuban Missile Crisis (1962), a new series of arms-control issues appeared, including the need for diplomatic communication to avert potential nuclear catastrophe. Beginning in the 1960s, the United States and the Soviet Union sponsored several international arms-control agreements designed to be of limited risk to each side. The first of these, the partial Nuclear Test-Ban Treaty (1963), prohibited tests of nuclear weapons in the atmosphere, in outer space, and underwater, which thus effectively confined nuclear explosions to underground sites. The Outer Space Treaty (1967) further limited the deployment of nuclear weapons and other weapons of mass destruction by banning countries from placing them in orbit. In 1968 the two superpowers took the lead in establishing the Treaty on the Non-proliferation of Nuclear Weapons (Non-proliferation Treaty; NPT), whereby they agreed not to promote the spread, or proliferation, of nuclear weapons to countries that did not already possess them. Two classes of states are parties to the NPT: those possessing nuclear weapons, such as China, France, Russia, the United Kingdom, and the United States, and nonnuclear states. The treaty, originally signed by 62 countries, had grown to some 185 parties by the early 21st century, although declared or suspected nuclear states such as India, Pakistan, and Israel were not parties. The NPT became effective in 1970 for a 25-year period; it was extended indefinitely in 1995.

THE CUBAN MISSILE CRISIS

In October 1962, the presence of Soviet nuclear-armed missiles in Cuba brought the United States and the Soviet Union close to war. Having promised in May 1960 to defend Cuba with Soviet arms, the Soviet premier, Nikita Khrushchev, assumed that the United States would take no steps to prevent the installation of Soviet medium- and intermediate-range ballistic missiles in Cuba. Such missiles could hit much of the eastern United States within a few minutes if launched from Cuba. The United States learned in July 1962 that the Soviet Union had begun missile shipments to Cuba. By August 29 new military construction and the presence of Soviet technicians had been reported by U.S. U-2 spy planes flying over the island, and on October 14 the presence of a ballistic missile on a launching site was reported.

After carefully considering the alternatives of an immediate U.S. invasion of Cuba (or air strikes of the missile sites), a blockade of the island, or further diplomatic maneuvers, Pres. John F. Kennedy decided to place a naval "quarantine," or blockade, on Cuba to prevent further Soviet shipments of missiles. Kennedy announced the quarantine on October 22 and warned that U.S. forces would seize "offensive weapons and associated matériel" that Soviet vessels might attempt to deliver to Cuba. During the following days, Soviet ships bound for Cuba altered course away from the quarantined zone. As the two superpowers hovered close to the brink of nuclear war, messages were exchanged between Kennedy and Khrushchev amidst extreme tension on both sides. On October 28 Khrushchev capitulated, informing Kennedy that work on the missile sites would be halted and that the missiles already in Cuba would be returned to the Soviet Union. In return, Kennedy committed the United States never to invade Cuba. Kennedy also discreetly agreed to withdraw nuclear-armed missiles that the United States had stationed in Turkey in previous years. In the following weeks both superpowers began fulfilling their promises, and the crisis was over by late November. Cuba's communist leader, Fidel Castro, was infuriated by the Soviets' retreat in the face of the U.S. ultimatum but was powerless to act.

The Cuban missile crisis marked the climax of an acutely antagonistic period in U.S.-Soviet relations. The crisis also

President John F. Kennedy announcing the U.S. naval blockade of Cuba on Oct. 22, 1962. © Archive Photos

marked the closest point that the world had ever come to global nuclear war. It is generally believed that the Soviets' humiliation in Cuba played an important part in Khrushchev's fall from power in October 1964 and in the Soviet Union's determination to achieve, at the least, a nuclear parity with the United States.

During the 1970s the Strategic Arms Limitation Talks (SALT) helped to restrain the continuing buildup by the Soviet Union and the United States of nuclear-armed intercontinental (long-range or strategic) ballistic missiles (ICBMs). One major part of the SALT I complex of agreements reached in 1972 severely limited each country's future deployment of antiballistic missiles (ABMs), which could be used to destroy incoming ICBMs. The Anti-Ballistic Missile Treaty (ABM Treaty) provided that each country could have no more than two ABM deployment areas and could not establish a nationwide system of ABM defense; a protocol to the agreement, signed in 1974, limited each party to a single ABM deployment area. The ABM Treaty, which was predicated on the strategy of mutually assured destruction, ensured that each side would remain vulnerable to the other's strategic offensive forces. Another part of the SALT I agreement froze the number of each side's ICBMs and submarine-launched ballistic missiles (SLBMs) at current levels. The SALT II agreement (1979) set limits on each side's store of multiple independent reentry vehicles (MIRVs), which were strategic missiles equipped with multiple nuclear warheads capable of hitting different targets on the ground. This agreement placed limits on the number of MIRVs, strategic bombers, and other strategic launchers each side possessed. Although the SALT agreements stabilized the nuclear arms race between the two superpowers, it did so at very high force levels, with each country continuing to possess many times the offensive capacity needed to utterly destroy the other in a nuclear exchange.

During the 1970s the United States and the Soviet Union also facilitated the establishment of the Convention on the Prohibition of the Development, Production and Stockpiling of Bacteriological (Biological) and Toxin Weapons and on Their Destruction (1972). Commonly known as the Biological Weapons Convention, the agreement supplemented the Geneva Protocol of 1925 and required all signatories both to refrain from developing and producing biological or toxin weapons and to destroy such weapons that they may possess that "have no justification for prophylactic, protective, and other peaceful purposes." Since it entered into force in 1975, the convention has been reviewed several times in order to take into account new scientific and technological developments, though there is no method in place to monitor compliance.

In 1985 the accession in the Soviet Union of a liberalizing regime under Mikhail Gorbachev generated intensified arms-control negotiations between the two superpowers. The result of these efforts, the Intermediate-Range Nuclear Forces Treaty (1987), committed the United States and the Soviet Union to the complete elimination of their stocks of intermediate- and medium-range land-based missiles. In the meantime, a new set of bilateral negotiations between the superpowers had begun in 1982 with the aim of reducing rather than merely limiting their arsenals of nuclear warheads and launch platforms (missiles and bombers). These negotiations, called the Strategic Arms Reduction Talks (START), produced a treaty in 1991 that committed the superpowers to reducing their strategic nuclear forces by 25 to 30 percent over a period of years. The United States and the Soviet Union also began eliminating various types of tactical (battlefield) nuclear-armed weapons, including artillery shells, depth charges, land mines, bombs, and the warheads carried on various tactical missiles.

AFTER THE COLD WAR

Following the breakup of the Soviet Union in late 1991, newly sovereign Russia undertook efforts to drastically reduce its nuclear and conventional armed forces through unilateral actions and agreements with the United States. The newly independent republics of Ukraine, Belarus, and Kazakhstan inherited some of the Soviet Union's nuclear arsenal but quickly pursued complete nuclear disarmament; all three became nuclear free by 1996. In 1992 an informal agreement (START II) was reached between the United States and Russia that would further drastically reduce each country's strategic nuclear forces over a period extending into the early 21st century.

In the 1990s the United States and Russia played major roles in the conclusion of the Chemical Weapons Convention (1993), which prohibited the development, production, stockpiling, and use of chemical weapons and called for the destruction of existing stocks within 10 years. The convention, drafted by the 39 countries of the Conference on Disarmament and entering into force in 1997, reaffirmed the Geneva Protocol of 1925, restated the prohibitions of the Treaty of Versailles (1919) and the Washington treaties (1921–22) against the use of poisonous gases, and added a ban on bacteriological warfare; 188 states were party to the agreement by 2010. The 1996 Comprehensive Nuclear-Test-Ban Treaty, which would prohibit all forms of nuclear explosive testing, had been signed by more than 165 states and ratified by more than 100 by the early 21st century but had failed to enter into force because some of the 44 states whose signatures and ratification were required for its enactment either chose to sign but not to ratify (e.g., the United States, China) or chose not to sign at all (India, North Korea, and Pakistan).

In June 2002, despite intense international opposition, the United States, citing fundamental changes in its security needs since the 1970s, withdrew from the ABM Treaty to pursue a national missile defense system designed to protect the country against nuclear attack. The United States subsequently offered to share defense technology with Russia and cover some of its allies, but the Russian response was lukewarm. Although Russia opposed the U.S. decision, its reaction was restrained; in May 2002, five months after the United States announced its intent to withdraw from the ABM Treaty, the two countries signed the Strategic Offensive Reductions Treaty (SORT), which committed each side to reducing its store of strategic nuclear warheads. Negotiations to replace the 1991 START I agreement, which established crucial trust-building verification procedures, began before the treaty's expiration in 2009. On April 8, 2010, the United States and Russia signed the New Strategic Arms Reduction Treaty (New START). Ratified by both countries by the following January, the new treaty would limit each country to 1,550 deployed strategic nuclear warheads.

MAJOR ARMS-CONTROL TREATIES

The major treaties intended to limit, reduce, or even abolish weapons of mass destruction are described below.

THE NUCLEAR TEST-BAN TREATY

The Treaty Banning Nuclear Weapons Tests in the Atmosphere, in Outer Space, and Under Water was signed in Moscow on Aug. 5, 1963, by the United States, the Soviet Union, and the United Kingdom. It banned all tests of nuclear weapons except those conducted underground.

The origins of the treaty lay in worldwide public concern over the danger posed by atmospheric radioactive fallout produced by the aboveground testing of nuclear weapons. This problem had

U.S. Pres. John F. Kennedy signing the Nuclear Test-Ban Treaty, Oct. 7, 1963. National Archives and Records Administration

become an important public issue by 1955, but the first negotiations to ban nuclear tests foundered on differing proposals and counterproposals made by the United States and the Soviet Union, which were the two dominant nuclear powers at the time. During most of 1959, both the United States and the Soviet Union temporarily suspended their testing, but negotiations over the next two years were slowed by renewed Cold War tensions between the two countries. A gradual rapprochement between the United States and the Soviet Union was speeded up by the Cuban Missile Crisis (October 1962), which vividly illustrated the dangers of nuclear confrontation. The Anglo-American and Soviet proposals for a draft treaty came to resemble one another during late 1962, and, after only 10 days of discussion in Moscow in July–August 1963, representatives of the three nuclear powers pledged themselves for an "unlimited duration" to conduct no more tests in the atmosphere, underwater, or in space.

The Nuclear Test-Ban Treaty banned nuclear-weapons tests in the atmosphere, in outer space, and underwater but permitted underground testing and required no control posts, no on-site inspection, and no international supervisory body. It did not reduce nuclear stockpiles, halt the production of nuclear weapons, or restrict their use in time of war. Within a few months of signing by the three original parties in August 1963, the treaty was signed by more than 100 other governments, notable exceptions being France and China. The three original parties to the treaty, the United States, the United Kingdom, and the Soviet Union (and its successor, Russia), have the power to veto treaty amendments. Any amendment must be approved by a majority of all the signatory states, including all three of the original parties.

It took until 1977 for negotiations to begin on a Comprehensive Nuclear-Test-Ban Treaty, which would extend the ban to underground tests, although the previous year the United States, the United Kingdom, and the Soviet Union had agreed to a treaty banning peaceful nuclear explosions—that is, those ostensibly conducted for purposes of civil engineering projects. Negotiations between the three powers continued until 1980. These faced considerable opposition in the United States, not least from the weapons laboratories, and in 1982 the administration of U.S. Pres. Ronald Reagan decided to abandon them. In 1991 the Soviet Union announced a moratorium on future nuclear tests, and the U.S. Congress required that this be reciprocated and that talks on a treaty resume. In 1994 the Ad Hoc Committee on a Nuclear Test Ban began negotiations under the auspices of the United Nations' Committee on Disarmament. A draft treaty banning all nuclear weapon test explosions and all peaceful nuclear explosions was passed by the UN General Assembly in 1996 and then was opened for signature. To enter into force, the Comprehensive Nuclear-Test-Ban Treaty has to be ratified by all the nuclear powers and by 44 members of the Conference on Disarmament that possess nuclear reactors. By 2011 all of these countries but three (India, Pakistan, and North Korea) had signed, though six of those that had signed had not ratified, including the United States and China.

Following the moratoriums of the early 1990s, Russia, the United States, the United Kingdom, and France conducted no further tests. France resumed testing briefly in 1995 and permanently ended testing only the following January. China conducted its last test on July 29, 1996. In 1998 both India and Pakistan tested nuclear weapons for the first time, although they also followed their tests with an informal moratorium. In October 2006 North Korea conducted its first test of a nuclear device, although the extremely small yield suggested that this might have been a failure. Another test followed in May 2009.

THE OUTER SPACE TREATY

The 1967 Treaty on Principles Governing the Activities of States in the Exploration and Use of Outer Space, Including the Moon and Other Celestial Bodies binds the parties to use outer space only for peaceful purposes. In June 1966 the United States and the Soviet Union submitted draft treaties on the uses of space to the United Nations. These were reconciled during several months of negotiation in the Legal Subcommittee of the UN Committee on the Peaceful Uses of Outer Space, and the resulting document was endorsed by the UN General Assembly on Dec. 19, 1966, and opened for signature on Jan. 27, 1967. The treaty came into force on Oct. 10, 1967, after being ratified by the United States, the Soviet Union, the United Kingdom, and several other countries.

Under the terms of the treaty, the parties are prohibited from placing nuclear arms or other weapons of mass destruction in orbit, on the Moon, or on other bodies in space. Nations cannot claim sovereignty over the Moon or other celestial bodies. Nations are responsible for their activities in space, are liable for any damage caused by objects launched into space from their territory, and are bound to assist astronauts in distress. Their space installations and vehicles shall be open, on a reciprocal basis, to representatives of other countries, and all parties agree to conduct outer-space activities openly and in accordance with international law.

THE NUCLEAR NON-PROLIFERATION TREATY

Under the terms of the Treaty on the Nonproliferation of Nuclear Weapons, signed on July 1, 1968, by the United Kingdom, the United States, the Soviet Union, and 59 other states, the three major signatories, which possessed nuclear weapons, agreed not to assist other states in obtaining or producing them. The treaty became effective in March 1970 and was to remain so for a 25-year period. Additional countries later ratified

British Foreign Secretary Michael Stewart signing the Treaty on the Non-proliferation of Nuclear Weapons, London, 1968.

the treaty; as of 2010 only three countries (India, Israel, and Pakistan) had refused to sign the treaty, and one country (North Korea) had signed and then withdrawn from the treaty. The treaty was extended indefinitely and without conditions in 1995 by a consensus vote of 174 countries at the United Nations headquarters in New York City.

The Non-proliferation Treaty is uniquely unequal, as it obliges non-nuclear states to forgo development of nuclear weapons while allowing the established nuclear states to keep theirs. Nevertheless, it has been accepted because, especially at the time of signing, most nonnuclear states had neither the capacity nor the inclination to follow the nuclear path, and they were well aware of the dangers of proliferation for their security. In addition, it was understood in 1968 that, in return for their special status, the nuclear states would help the nonnuclear states in the development of civilian nuclear power (although in the event the distinction between civilian and military nuclear technology was not so straightforward) and that the nuclear states would make their best efforts to agree on measures of disarmament. In the 2005 Review Conference of the Parties to the Treaty on Non-proliferation of Nuclear Weapons, this inequality was a major complaint against the established nuclear powers. The treaty continues to play an important role in sustaining the international norm against proliferation, but it has been challenged by a number of events, including (1) North Korea's withdrawal from the treaty in 2003 as it sought to acquire nuclear weapons, (2) evidence of the progress Iraq made in the 1980s on its nuclear program despite being a signatory to the treaty, and (3) allegations about uranium enrichment facilities in Iran, yet another signatory to the treaty. The credibility of the nonproliferation norm has also been undermined by the ability of India and Pakistan to become declared nuclear powers in 1998 without any serious international penalty—and indeed by India establishing its own special arrangements as part of a bilateral deal in 2008 to cooperate on civilian nuclear technology with the United States, a signatory party to the treaty.

THE STRATEGIC ARMS LIMITATION TALKS

SALT was a series of negotiations between the United States and the Soviet Union that were aimed at curtailing the manufacture of strategic missiles capable of carrying nuclear weapons. The first agreements, known as SALT I and SALT II, were signed by the United States and the Union of Soviet Socialist Republics in 1972 and 1979, respectively, and were intended to restrain the arms race in strategic (long-range or intercontinental) ballistic missiles armed with nuclear weapons. First suggested by U.S. Pres. Lyndon B. Johnson in 1967, strategic arms limitation talks were agreed on by the two superpowers in the summer of 1968, and full-scale negotiations began in November 1969.

Of the resulting complex of agreements (SALT I), the most important were the ABM Treaty and the Interim Agreement and Protocol on Limitation of Strategic Offensive Weapons. Both were signed by Pres. Richard M. Nixon for the United States and Leonid Brezhnev, general secretary of the Soviet Communist Party, for the U.S.S.R. on May 26, 1972, at a summit meeting in Moscow.

The ABM treaty regulated antiballistic missiles that could theoretically be used to destroy incoming ICBMs launched by the other superpower. The treaty limitations prevented either party from defending more than a small fraction of its entire territory, and thus kept both sides subject to the deterrent effect of the other's strategic forces. The ABM treaty was ratified by the U.S. Senate on Aug. 3, 1972. The Interim Agreement froze each side's number of ICBMs and SLBMs at current levels for five years, pending negotiation of a more detailed SALT II. As an executive agreement, it did not require U.S. Senate ratification, but it was approved by Congress in a joint resolution.

The SALT II negotiations opened late in 1972 and continued for seven years. A basic problem in these negotiations was the asymmetry between the strategic forces of the two countries, the U.S.S.R. having concentrated on missiles with large warheads while the United States had developed smaller missiles of greater accuracy. Questions also arose as to new technologies under development, matters of definition, and methods of verification.

As finally negotiated, the SALT II treaty set limits on the number of strategic launchers (i.e., missiles that could be equipped with multiple independently targetable reentry vehicles [MIRVs]), with the object of deferring the time when both sides' land-based ICBM systems would become vulnerable to attack from such missiles. Limits were put on the number of MIRVed ICBMs, MIRVed SLBMs, heavy (i.e., long-range) bombers, and the total number of strategic launchers. The treaty set an overall limit of about 2,400 of all such weapons systems for each side. The SALT II treaty was signed by Pres. Jimmy Carter and Brezhnev in Vienna on June 18, 1979, and was submitted to the U.S. Senate for ratification shortly thereafter. But renewed tensions between the superpowers prompted Carter to remove the treaty from Senate consideration in January 1980, after the Soviet Union's invasion of Afghanistan. The United States and the Soviet Union voluntarily observed the arms limits agreed upon in SALT II in subsequent years, however. Meanwhile, the renewed negotiations that opened between the two superpowers in Geneva in 1982 took the name of Strategic Arms Reduction Talks, or START.

THE ABM TREATY

The Treaty on the Limitation of Anti-Ballistic Missile Systems was an arms-control treaty ratified in 1972 between the United States and the Soviet Union to limit deployment of missile systems that could theoretically be used to destroy incoming ICBMs launched by the other superpower. Negotiations to prohibit ballistic missile defenses were first proposed by the United States in 1966 but did not begin until late 1969, as part of SALT. The ABM Treaty was signed by U.S. Pres. Richard Nixon and Soviet leader Leonid Brezhnev at a summit in Moscow in May 1972, and it was ratified by both the U.S. Senate and the Supreme Soviet later that year.

The ABM Treaty limited each side to only two ABM deployment areas, one to protect the national capital and another to protect an ICBM launch site, with each ABM deployment area limited to 100 launch systems and 100 interceptor missiles. A 1974 protocol reduced the agreement to one ABM site apiece. The Soviet Union opted to maintain an established system protecting Moscow; it was upgraded in the 1980s and remained officially operational into the post-Soviet period, though most observers concluded that it had declined considerably by the end of the 1990s. The United States opted to protect an ICBM site at Grand Forks, N.D., although the system deployed was decommissioned in 1976. To prevent the deployment of a nationwide battle management system, the treaty required all early-warning radars (usually large phased-array radars) to be sited on the periphery of the country, oriented outward. In 1984 the United States claimed that a Soviet radar system near the city of Krasnoyarsk, 800 km (500 miles) from the nearest border, violated this provision, and in 1989 the Soviets acknowledged the violation and agreed to dismantle the radar. In addition to traditional interceptor missiles, launchers, and radars, the ABM Treaty also covered systems based on other principles, such as lasers.

Under the terms of the treaty, neither party was able to defend more than a small fraction of its entire territory, and both sides were thus kept subject to the deterrent effect of the other's strategic forces. This arrangement was seen to reinforce the concept of mutual assured destruction (MAD), in which the prospect of annihilation for both sides would prevent either side from "going nuclear" in the event of a conflict. The very concept of MAD was controversial, however. During the 1980s, U.S. Pres. Ronald Reagan promoted his Strategic Defense Initiative (also known as Star Wars), based on an alternative concept of assured survival. Technology existing at the time did not support this ambitious goal, though, and in any case the end of the Cold War

significantly lowered the risk of a massive nuclear exchange. During the course of the 1990s, attention turned to the risk of small-scale missile attacks from so-called "rogue" states, such as North Korea or Iraq. With this in mind, a National Missile Defense (NMD) system was proposed in the United States. Although it would involve no more than 100 interceptors, it was a system designed to provide nationwide defense and so would be inconsistent with the ABM Treaty. For this reason, Russia publicly opposed the NMD. In order to mollify the Russians, the administration of U.S. Pres. Bill Clinton explored amending the ABM Treaty during the 1990s to permit the deployment of limited defenses that would clearly not be able to blunt a Russian attack. The administration of U.S. Pres. George W. Bush, however, saw no merit in trying to preserve a treaty that it described as a "relic" of the Cold War era, and in December 2001 Bush gave the required six-months notice of abrogation of the ABM Treaty, which was the first time that the United States had withdrawn from a major arms control agreement. Russia did no more than describe this action as "mistaken."

THE INF TREATY

The Intermediate-Range Nuclear Forces Treaty, a nuclear-arms-control accord reached by the United States and the Soviet Union in 1987, obliged those two countries to eliminate their stocks of intermediate-range and shorter-range (or "medium-range") land-based missiles (which could carry nuclear warheads). It was the first arms-control treaty to abolish an entire category of weapon systems. In addition, two protocols to the treaty established unprecedented procedures for observers from both nations to verify firsthand the other nation's destruction of its missiles.

The INF Treaty defined intermediate-range ballistic missiles (IRBMs) and ground-launched cruise missiles (GLCMs) as those having ranges of 1,000 to 5,500 km (620 to 3,400 miles) and shorter-range ballistic missiles (SRBMs) as those having ranges from 500 to 1,000 km.

The deployment of IRBMs in Europe first became an arms-control issue in the late 1970s, when the Soviet Union began replacing its older single-warhead SS-4 and SS-5 IRBMs with newer and more accurate SS-20s, which could deliver three nuclear warheads apiece from a distance of 5,000 km. Mounted on mobile launchers based in the European part of the Soviet Union, the SS-20s could strike targets anywhere in western Europe in less than 10 minutes.

Under pressure from its western European allies in NATO, the United States in 1979 committed itself to deploying two intermediate-range weapons systems of its own in western Europe: the Pershing II and the Tomahawk cruise missile. Mounted on mobile launchers, the Pershing II was an IRBM that could carry a single nuclear warhead a distance of about 2,000 km and strike within the vicinity of Moscow in less than 10 minutes.

The SS-20 and the Pershing II could deliver warheads to their targets with unprecedented accuracy. They thus had the capability to destroy reinforced command bunkers and missile silos deep within enemy territory. Such missiles, it was argued, were not defensive in nature but were actually destabilizing "first-strike" weapons that directly threatened both the military command structure of NATO and prime targets within the Soviet heartland. This created the political incentive for both sides to curtail such weapons through arms-control negotiations.

INF negotiations began in October 1980, three years after the first SS-20s were deployed in the Soviet Union and three years before the first Pershings and Tomahawks were deployed in western Europe under NATO auspices. The treaty as finally approved was based upon the "zero option" proposed by the United States in November 1981. Under this proposal, NATO would forgo deploying its intermediate-range missiles if the Soviets dismantled their SS-20s and the older IRBMs it was replacing. After five years of interrupted and often acrimonious negotiation, the Soviet Union accepted the concept of elimination (rather than mere reduction) of all land-based IRBMs and, in July 1987, expanded it to include a "double-zero" option. This proposal called for the elimination not only of all of the superpowers' intermediate-range missiles but also of their shorter-range missiles as well. These SRBMs consisted of the U.S. Pershing 1A and the Soviet SS-12 and SS-23. The United States agreed to this proposal. The Soviet Union also agreed to on-site verification of the missiles' destruction.

The treaty incorporating these commitments was signed in Washington, D.C., on Dec. 8, 1987, by U.S. Pres. Ronald Reagan and Soviet General Secretary Mikhail Gorbachev. It was ratified by the U.S. Senate and the Supreme Soviet the following year.

The INF Treaty called for the progressive dismantling, over three years, of 2,619 missiles, about half of which were deployed at the time of signing. About two-thirds of the missiles affected were Soviet, and the rest were American. Each country was allowed to keep intact the warheads and guidance systems of the destroyed missiles. Also destroyed were missile launchers and various kinds of support equipment and structures. Teams of observers from both countries were given access to certain operating bases, support facilities, and elimination facilities in order to verify the withdrawal and destruction of the missile systems. In order to ensure the permanent elimination of intermediate-range missiles, each country was given the right for 13 years to conduct periodic inspections of operating bases and support facilities and to monitor one production plant at which weapons of the INF category might be produced.

THE STRATEGIC ARMS REDUCTION TALKS

START is a series of arms control negotiations between the United States and the Soviet Union (and, later, Russia) that were aimed at reducing those two countries' arsenals of nuclear warheads and of the missiles and bombers capable of delivering such weapons. The talks, which began in 1982, spanned a period of three eventful decades that saw the collapse of the Soviet Union, the end of the Cold War, and the major crises of the early 21st century.

START I

The START negotiations were successors to the Strategic Arms Limitation Talks of the 1970s. In resuming strategic-arms negotiations with the Soviet Union in 1982, U.S. Pres. Ronald Reagan renamed the talks START and proposed radical reductions, rather than merely limitations, in each superpower's existing stocks of missiles and warheads. In 1983 the Soviet Union abandoned arms control talks in protest against the deployment of intermediate-range missiles in western Europe. In 1985 START resumed, and the talks culminated in July 1991 with a comprehensive strategic-arms-reduction agreement signed by U.S. Pres. George H.W. Bush and Soviet leader Mikhail Gorbachev. The new treaty was ratified without difficulty in the U.S. Senate, but in December 1991 the Soviet Union broke up, leaving in its wake four independent republics with strategic nuclear weapons—Belarus, Kazakhstan, Ukraine, and Russia. In May 1992 the Lisbon Protocol was signed, which allowed for all four to become parties to START I and for Ukraine, Belarus, and Kazakhstan either to destroy their strategic nuclear warheads or to turn them over to Russia. This made possible ratification by the new Russian Duma, although not before yet another agreement had been reached with Ukraine setting the terms for the transfer of all the nuclear warheads on its territory to Russia. All five START I parties exchanged the instruments of ratification in Budapest on Dec. 5, 1994.

The START I treaty set limits to be reached in a first phase within three years and then a second phase within five years. By the end of the second phase, in 1999, both the United States and Russia would be permitted a total of 7,950 warheads on a maximum of 1,900 delivery vehicles (missiles and bombers). This limit involved reductions from established levels of about 11,000 warheads on each side. Of the 7,950 permitted warheads, no more than 6,750 could be mounted on deployed ICBMs and SLBMs. The treaty included demanding verification measures, including on-site inspection, monitors at the Russian mobile ICBM factory at Votkinsk, and access to missile telemetry, which provides details of the characteristics of missiles being tested. By early 1997 Belarus and Kazakhstan had reached zero nuclear warheads, and Ukraine destroyed its last ICBMs in 1999.

The United States and Russia reached the required levels for the second phase during 1997.

A third phase was to be completed by the end of 2001, when both sides were to get down to 6,000 warheads on a maximum of 1,600 delivery vehicles, with no more than 4,900 warheads on deployed ICBMs and SLBMs. Although there had been concerns that this goal would not be achieved because of the expense and difficulty of decommissioning weapons, both sides enacted their cuts by 2001. The START I treaty expired on Dec. 5, 2009.

During the negotiations on START I, one of the most controversial issues had been how to handle limits on nuclear-armed cruise missiles, as verification would be difficult to implement. The issue was finally handled by means of separate political declarations by which the two sides agreed to announce annually their planned cruise missile deployments, which were not to exceed 880.

START II

Even as they agreed on the outline of START I in 1990, the United States and the Soviet Union accepted that further reductions should be negotiated. However, real negotiations had to wait for the elections that established the leadership of the new Russian Federation in 1992. The START II treaty was agreed on at two summit meetings between George H.W. Bush and Russian Pres. Boris Yeltsin, the first in Washington, D.C., in June 1992 and the second in Moscow in January 1993.

Under its terms, both sides would reduce their strategic warheads to 3,800–4,250 by 2000 and to 3,000–3,500 by 2003. They would also eliminate MIRVs on their ICBMs—in effect eliminating two of the more controversial missiles of the Cold War, the U.S. Peacekeeper missile and the Russian SS-18. Later, in order to accommodate the delays in signing and ratifying START I, the deadlines were put back to 2004 and 2007, respectively.

START II never actually came into force. The U.S. Senate did not ratify the treaty until 1996, largely because the parallel process was moving so slowly in the Russian Duma. There the treaty became a hostage to growing Russian irritation with Western policies in the Persian Gulf and the Balkans and then to concerns over American attitudes toward the ABM Treaty. The Russian preference would have been for far lower final levels, as Russia lacked the resources to replace many of its aging weapons systems, but achieved at a slower pace, because it also lacked the resources for speedy decommissioning. In 2000 the Duma linked the fate of START II to the ABM Treaty, and in June 2002, following the United States' withdrawal from the ABM Treaty, the Duma repudiated START II.

START III/SORT

Part of the Duma's objection was that the proposed cuts were not deep enough. A more radical treaty therefore might have a better chance of ratification. In March 1997, U.S. Pres. Bill Clinton and Yeltsin agreed to begin negotiating START III, which would bring each side down to 2,000–2,500 warheads by Dec. 31, 2007. Discussions then got bogged down over the ABM Treaty, as the Russians sought to link reductions on offensive systems with the maintenance of the established restraints on defensive systems. Nonetheless, it still suited both sides to demonstrate progress, and the risks of agreement were limited by making provisions reversible if circumstances changed. Proposals from both sides began to converge in 2001, and on May 24, 2002, U.S. Pres. George W. Bush and Russian Pres. Vladimir Putin signed the Strategic Offensive Reductions Treaty (SORT). That treaty, sometimes referred to as the Moscow Treaty, was ratified without difficulty by both the U.S. Senate and the Russian Duma, in March and May 2003, respectively.

SORT would reduce strategic nuclear weapons to between 1,700 and 2,200 warheads by Dec. 31, 2012. It did not require the elimination of delivery systems; it allowed nondeployed warheads to be stored instead of destroyed; and for verification it relied on mechanisms outlined in START I. Implementation of SORT proceeded without problems, although it was apparent from the beginning that difficulties might arise if START I were to lapse on schedule in 2009 without replacement. Agreement to negotiate a replacement to START I was made difficult by tensions on a range of issues, including the United States' occupation of Iraq in 2003, Russia's invasion of

Georgia in 2008, and U.S. plans to install ballistic missile defense systems in eastern Europe in order to deter a potential threat from Iran's growing missile force.

NEW START

By early 2009, however, agreement between the two sides was possible, with a new administration in Washington under Pres. Barack Obama. Negotiations continued through the formal expiration of START I in December, and Obama and Russian Pres. Dmitry Medvedev agreed to work out a new treaty by December that would build on the verification arrangements of START I and reduce strategic weapons on each side to 500–1,000 warheads and 1,500–1,675 delivery systems. The negotiations proved to be more difficult than anticipated, but by April 8, 2010, agreement was reached on a new treaty that would limit each side to 1,550 deployed strategic warheads on up to 800 strategic nuclear delivery vehicles (deployed and nondeployed). Under the new treaty, no more than 700 of the delivery vehicles would be deployed ballistic missile launchers and nuclear-armed bombers; the rest would be systems for training and testing or launchers without missiles. Outside these limits, there was freedom to mix types of systems to suit the two sides' respective force structures.

The targets set by the so-called New START are some 30 percent below the levels set by SORT in 2002. The new limits must be reached seven years after ratification by the Senate (which came in December 2010) and the Duma (which voted to ratify in January 2011). The verification procedures of START I have been streamlined to do away with redundant monitoring procedures—for instance, ending the permanent monitoring at Votkinsk and reducing telemetry access. The New START does, however, call for more on-site inspections.

THE BIOLOGICAL WEAPONS CONVENTION

The Convention on the Prohibition of the Development, Production and Stockpiling of Bacteriological (Biological) and Toxin Weapons and on Their Destruction (frequently referred to simply as the Biological Weapons Convention, or BWC) is an international treaty that bans the use of biological weapons in war and also prohibits all development, production, acquisition, stockpiling, or transfer of such weapons. The convention was signed in London, Moscow, and Washington, D.C., on April 10, 1972, and thereafter was opened for signing by other states. The convention went into force on March 26, 1975, following the submission of 22 national instruments of ratification (such as passage by a national assembly). By 2010, 177 states and Taiwan had signed the BWC, and 163 of these states plus Taiwan had ratified it.

The BWC prohibits countries that have signed the treaty from developing, producing, stockpiling, acquiring, or retaining biological agents or toxins of types and in quantities that have no justification for protective, defensive, or other peaceful purposes. The treaty also bans any equipment or means of delivery that is designed to use biological agents or toxins for hostile purposes or armed conflict. It requires signatories to destroy biological weapons, agents, and production facilities within nine months of the treaty's entry into force.

Unfortunately, the BWC does not yet contain provisions for verification of members' compliance, and there has been evidence of significant cheating by some parties since the treaty went into effect. For example, the Soviet Union engaged in a massive clandestine biological weapons program in direct violation of the BWC from the day it signed the treaty in 1972. The illegal program was revealed by scientists formerly involved in the program and finally confirmed by Russia's first post-Soviet president, Boris Yeltsin, who ordered the termination of all Russian offensive biological weapons programs in 1992.

The lack of a necessarily intrusive inspection and reporting system has left the states who are parties to the treaty with no strong assurance that they can monitor and verify other members' compliance with the terms of the BWC. Biological weapons programs can be easily concealed and need not require large numbers of personnel or large-scale physical plants. For instance, a clandestine weapons program can be hidden inside a perfectly legal vaccine-production facility or pharmaceutical plant. Weapons laboratories disguised in this way would give off few unique "signatures," or tell-tale signs that illicit activity is taking place. Indeed, if "national technical means" (that is, spy satellites and other such systems) are the only methods used to verify BWC compliance, and if more-traditional "human intelligence" (i.e., spies and defectors) is insufficient, a massive biological weapons program might take place in a country that has signed the BWC without any physical evidence's coming to light. This lack of a verification procedure has led some critics of the BWC to argue that the best deterrent to being attacked with biological weapons is not a treaty at all but rather the recognized ability to retaliate in equal or greater measure.

Proponents of the BWC argue that the treaty provides an international norm for the world community, making it understood by all that biological weapons are illegitimate tools of statecraft or warfare. Therefore, if violations are detected, the international community can be more easily mobilized to pressure the offending regime into giving up the weapons lest it face military, economic, and diplomatic sanctions. The BWC, it is also argued, makes proliferation harder, slower, and more expensive for cheaters. Finally, it is argued that the presence of an international treaty on biological weapons may put pressure on even non-signatory states to comply with the treaty or at least to restrict their biological weapons programs by creating an international norm against them.

THE CHEMICAL WEAPONS CONVENTION

The Convention on the Prohibition of the Development, Production, Stockpiling and Use of Chemical Weapons and on Their Destruction (better known simply as the Chemical Weapons Convention, or CWC) is an international treaty that bans the use of chemical weapons in war and also prohibits all development, production, acquisition, stockpiling, or transfer of such weapons. The CWC was adopted by the United Nations Conference on Disarmament on Sept. 3, 1992, and the treaty was opened to signature by all states on Jan. 13, 1993. The CWC entered into force on April 29, 1997. As of 2010, the only countries that had neither signed nor acceded to the CWC were Angola, Egypt, North Korea, Somalia, and Syria.

NEGOTIATING A TREATY

For almost a century before the CWC, a number of attempts had been made to limit or ban the use of chemical weapons in war. At the initiative of Nicholas II, emperor of Russia, delegates from around the world met at the 1899 and 1907 International Peace Conferences at The Hague. At the 1899 conference, the delegates agreed to prohibit the use of asphyxiating gases. Signatory states at both conferences agreed to prohibit the use of poison.

However, once chemical warfare was introduced on the battlefield by the German army in 1915, chemical weapons were produced and employed by all the powers participating in World War I, and more than a million chemical casualties and an estimated 91,000 fatalities resulted. Following the war, Germany was forbidden to manufacture or import poison gas munitions under the terms of the Treaty of Versailles (1919).

In 1925, at the initiative of the U.S. government, a diplomatic conference was called in Geneva, and a multinational protocol was negotiated and signed by most states prohibiting the use of poison gas and biological weapons in war. Ironically, the United States did not sign the protocol until 1975, owing to domestic opposition and a feeling that the protocol did not go far enough.

The 1925 Geneva Protocol banned the use of chemical and biological weapons but did not prohibit the development, production, stockpiling, or transfer of such weapons. Moreover, 25 of the signatory states reserved the right to retaliate in kind if another state used chemical weapons first. In reality, most of the powers that had signed the protocol had robust chemical warfare capabilities at the ready for use entering World War II, and all but Japan were deterred from use by the possession of such weapons by their adversaries.

After World War II, general multinational disarmament negotiations took place at the United Nations, including further discussions of limits to be put on chemical and biological weapons. Proposals were discussed at the Eighteen-Nation Disarmament Conference from 1962 to 1968 and then later in the UN Conference on Disarmament. Biological and chemical arms control were addressed separately. First to be addressed was biological disarmament, and this led to the negotiation, signature, and ratification of the Biological Weapons Convention in 1972.

After 1972 UN negotiators turned to chemical disarmament. In 1984 the United States tabled for consideration the first comprehensive detailed draft treaty by a major power. Real consensus had been blocked for a number of years by Cold War politics, and it was not until after Mikhail Gorbachev became general secretary of the Communist Party in 1985 that the Soviet Union began to also embrace comprehensive chemical arms control. By 1987 the two superpowers had begun to share a common perspective. While simultaneously working on a multilateral treaty, the United States and the Soviet Union, in a 1990 summit, also negotiated bilateral reductions of their chemical weapons. Each side agreed to reduce its stockpile to 5,000 tons of chemical agents.

With support finally coming from the United States and Russia (following the breakup of the Soviet Union), the UN Conference on Disarmament adopted the CWC treaty on Sept. 3, 1992, and the treaty was opened to signature by all states on Jan. 13, 1993. The CWC entered into force on April 29, 1997, 180 days after the deposit of the 65th instrument of ratification.

AIMS AND TERMS OF THE TREATY

The aim of the CWC is total chemical weapons disarmament. Signatory states that possess chemical weapons at the time they sign and ratify the treaty must destroy those arms and their production facilities. States members are also required to destroy any chemical weapons they may have abandoned on the territory of other countries.

In Article II of the CWC, chemical weapons are defined as all toxic chemicals intended for wartime use, which includes not only the finished weapons but also their chemical precursors, munitions, delivery devices, and any other equipment specifically designed for wartime use.

Certain kinds of toxic chemicals are, however, permitted by the CWC. These include those designed for peaceful uses, such as in experiments to test chemical protection equipment. There are also certain gray areas in the treaty that are open to interpretation. For example, riot-control agents such as tear gas are prohibited as a method of warfare, but they are permitted if designed strictly for law-enforcement purposes.

Chemicals to be controlled by the CWC are divided among three lists, or "schedules." Schedule 1 lists those chemicals considered to pose a high risk to the goals of the CWC, including precursor chemicals used to produce nerve agents or mustard agents. Schedule 2 lists those chemicals that generally are not produced in large commercial quantities for nonmilitary purposes and pose a significant risk to the purpose of the CWC. Finally, those listed in Schedule 3 are dual-use chemicals that are thought to pose a risk to the aims of the CWC but also have many legitimate commercial purposes and are produced worldwide in large amounts.

ENSURING COMPLIANCE

The CWC is administered by the Organisation for the Prohibition of Chemical Weapons (OPCW), headquartered at The Hague. Day-to-day affairs are conducted by the OPCW's Executive Council, which reports to the CWC's Conference of States Parties. This latter body in turn has responsibility for taking "the necessary measures to ensure compliance" and for administering penalties against signatory states that violate the terms of the CWC. The OPCW Technical Secretariat is responsible for carrying out various verification procedures to ensure that members comply with the agreement.

CWC verification is accomplished by a variety of means, including reporting requirements by the member states, OPCW inspections to determine a baseline for comparison with later inspections, regular on-site inspections, and challenge inspections. Any single party to the pact can request a challenge inspection of any other signatory party. Inspectors are to be given unimpeded access to all parts

of actual or suspected chemical weapons storage sites or to chemical production or destruction facilities. OPCW inspectors are permitted by the treaty to use continuous on-site monitoring devices and may use seals to ensure that a facility is not being used. The OPCW Technical Secretariat must give a member state prior notice of an impending regular inspection to a storage site. Sites that previously produced or are presently known or suspected to be storage areas for Schedule 1 chemical weapons or agents receive the most scrutiny.

Within 12 hours of receiving a challenge inspection request, the Executive Council of the OPCW may block the inspection if three-fourths or more of the 41 members on the Council are convinced that the request is frivolous or abusive. The director-general of the OPCW is required to formally notify the party to be inspected no less than 12 hours prior to the planned arrival of the inspection team. A series of rules then apply as to how inspectors can gain access to facilities in order to check compliance with CWC restrictions.

Each party to the accord is required to pass national implementing legislation to make it illegal for organizations or individuals in their jurisdiction to conduct activities prohibited by the CWC, such as the use, development, production, acquisition, stockpiling, or transfer of chemical arms.

CONCLUSION

The term *weapons of mass destruction* can be traced to at least 1937, when it was used to describe massed formations of bomber aircraft—weapons that, under Allied control, would carry out devastating firebombing raids on Germany and Japan during World War II. Yet a single atomic bomb dropped on Hiroshima from a U.S. airplane on Aug. 6, 1945, demonstrated that a weapon of mass destruction could result from a mere 64 kg (140 pounds) of uranium. The detonation of Little Boy opened the era of modern weapons of mass destruction.

During the Cold War, the United States, the Soviet Union, and other major powers built up enormous stockpiles containing tens of thousands of nuclear bombs, missile warheads, and artillery shells—so many that the military and diplomatic standoff of that era was sometimes described as a "balance of terror." As the Cold War came to a close, attention turned increasingly to proliferation—that is, the potential for lesser powers, "rogue states," or international terrorist groups to acquire the means to produce and deliver these weapons. Despite the array of international agreements that resulted, however, it became clear by the end of the 20th century that no treaty or convention could by itself prevent a weapon of mass destruction from falling into the hands of any state or group.

Whereas the United States and the Soviet Union once used huge numbers of missiles to threaten each other with massive retaliation and mutual assured destruction, today the pursuit of weapons of mass destruction takes a variety of forms, from conventional war between nation-states to the cat-and-mouse games of cyberwarfare. What has remained consistent is the belief that the very presence of a weapon of mass destruction in the hands of a hostile power is a grievous threat that must be confronted.

airburst The burst of a shell or bomb in the air.

centrifuge A machine using centrifugal force for separating substances of different densities, for removing moisture, or for simulating gravitational effects.

clemency Disposition to be merciful and especially to moderate the severity of punishment due.

critical Of sufficient size (as a mass of fissionable material) to sustain a chain reaction.

critical mass The mass of fissile material required to produce a chain reaction.

cruise missile A guided missile usually propelled by a jet engine that flies at moderate speed and low altitude.

cyclotron An accelerator in which charged particles (as protons, deuterons, or ions) are propelled by an alternating electric field in a constant magnetic field.

depth charge An antisubmarine weapon that consists essentially of a drum filled with explosives that is dropped near a target and descends to a predetermined depth where it explodes.

détente The relaxation of strained relations or tensions (as between nations).

dynamic pressure The quantity of air measured by most airspeed instruments and equal to the product $1/2\rho V^2$

where ρ is the density of the air and V is the relative speed of the air.

electromagnetic pulse High-intensity electromagnetic radiation generated by a nuclear blast high above Earth's surface and held to disrupt electronic and electrical systems.

electrostatic repulsive force Attraction or repulsion of particles or objects because of their electric charge.

extradite To surrender an alleged criminal usually under the provisions of a treaty or statute by one authority (as a state) to another having jurisdiction to try the charge.

fallout The often radioactive particles stirred up by or resulting from a nuclear explosion and descending through the atmosphere.

firestorm A large usually stationary fire characterized by very high temperatures in which the central column of rising heated air induces strong inward winds that supply oxygen to the fire.

fissile Capable of undergoing fission by both fast and slow neutrons.

fission The splitting of an atomic nucleus resulting in the release of large amounts of energy.

force de frappe A "striking force," most commonly referring to the nuclear forces of France.

fusion The union of atomic nuclei to form heavier nuclei resulting in the release of enormous quantities of energy when certain light elements unite.

half-life The time required for half of the atoms of a radioactive substance to become disintegrated.

hardening Procedures designed to protect against blast, heat, or radiation (as by a thick barrier or placement underground).

irradiate To affect or treat by radiant energy (as heat).

isotope Any of two or more species of atoms of a chemical element with the same atomic number and nearly identical chemical behaviour but with differing atomic mass or mass number and different physical properties.

leitmotiv A dominant recurring theme.

mass spectograph An instrument used to separate and often to determine the masses of isotopes.

neutron An uncharged atomic particle that has a mass nearly equal to that of the proton and is present in all known atomic nuclei except the hydrogen nucleus.

nuclear winter The chilling of climate that is hypothesized to be a consequence of nuclear war and to result from the prolonged blockage of sunlight by high-altitude dust clouds produced by nuclear explosions.

overpressure Pressure significantly above what is usual or normal.

radiation Energy radiated in the form of waves or particles.

samizdat Government-suppressed literature from the Union of Soviet Socialist Republics and countries within its orbit that was clandestinely printed and distributed.

shock wave A compressional wave of high amplitude caused by a shock (as from an earthquake or explosion) to the medium through which the wave travels.

subcritical Of insufficient size (as a mass of fissionable material) to sustain a chain reaction.

supercritical Capable of carrying on a chain reaction in such a manner that the rate of reaction increases; used especially of fissionable material.

telemetry Highly automated communications process by which measurements are made and other data collected at remote or inaccessible points and transmitted to receiving equipment for monitoring, display, and recording.

thermal radiation Quantized electromagnetic radiation excited by thermal agitation of molecules or atoms and having a range including infrared, visible light, and ultraviolet.

thermonuclear Of, relating to, or employing transformations in the nuclei of atoms of low atomic weight (as hydrogen) that require a very high temperature for their inception (as in the hydrogen bomb or in the sun).

torpedo A weapon for destroying ships by rupturing their hulls below the waterline.

BIBLIOGRAPHY

NUCLEAR WEAPONS

The history of nuclear weapons is the subject of a voluminous literature. Richard Rhodes, *The Making of the Atomic Bomb* (1986), is the standard work on the development of the first American bomb, with an emphasis on the scientists involved in the effort. A counterbalance that describes the industrial, engineering, and administrative aspects is Robert S. Norris, *Racing for the Bomb: General Leslie R. Groves, the Manhattan Project's Indispensable Man* (2002). Lillian Hoddeson et al., *Critical Assembly: A Technical History of Los Alamos During the Oppenheimer Years, 1943–1945* (1993), is excellent on the technical aspects of developing the first nuclear weapons. These can be supplemented by the following official histories: Vincent C. Jones, *Manhattan, the Army and the Atomic Bomb* (1985); David Hawkins, Edith C. Truslow, and Ralph Carlisle Smith, *Manhattan District History—Project Y, the Los Alamos Project*, 2 vol. (1961, reprinted as *Project Y, the Los Alamos Story*, in 1 vol. with a new introduction, 1983); and Richard G. Hewlett, Oscar E. Anderson, Jr., and Francis Duncan, *A History of the United States Atomic Energy Commission*, 2 vol. (1962–69); continued by Richard G. Hewlett and Jack M. Holl, *Atoms for Peace and War, 1953–1961* (1989).

The development of thermonuclear weapons is discussed in Richard Rhodes, *Dark Sun* (1995); Herbert F. York, *The Advisors: Oppenheimer, Teller, and the Superbomb* (1976); and Hans A. Bethe, "Comments on the History of the H-Bomb," *Los Alamos Science*, 3(3):43–53 (Fall 1982).

The British project is discussed in the official histories of the U.K. Atomic Energy Authority: Margaret Gowing, *Britain and Atomic Energy, 1939–1945* (1964), and *Independence and Deterrence: Britain and Atomic Energy, 1945–1952*, 2 vol. (1974). Humphrey Wynn, *The RAF Strategic Nuclear Deterrent Forces: Their Origins, Roles, and Deployment, 1946–1969: A Documentary History* (1994), is an essential source. Lorna Arnold, *Britain and the H-Bomb* (2001), fills an important gap in information on thermonuclear weapons.

Since the demise of the Soviet Union, important information about its fission and fusion programs has been published by Russian and Western authors, including David Holloway, *Stalin and the Bomb: The Soviet Union and Atomic Energy, 1939–1956,* (1994); Thomas B. Cochran, Robert S. Norris, and Oleg A. Bukharin, *Making the Russian Bomb: From Stalin to Yeltsin*

(1995); and Pavel Podvig (ed.), *Russian Strategic Nuclear Forces* (2001).

No official history is available for the French project. Bertrand Goldschmidt, *Les Rivalités atomiques, 1939–1966* (1967), is a semiofficial account by a participant. André Bendjebbar, *Histoire secrète de la bombe atomique française* (2000), uses the archives and takes the story to 1962. Pierre Billaud, *La Véridique Histoire de la Bombe H française* (1994), and "Comment la France a fait sa Bombe H," *La Recherche*, 293:74–78 (December 1996), provide important details. Declan Butler, "Did UK Scientist Give France Vital Clues About H-Bomb?" *Nature*, 384(6608):392 (Dec. 5, 1996), discusses the revelations.

The Chinese project is covered in John Wilson Lewis and Xue Litai, *China Builds the Bomb* (1988); and Robert S. Norris, Andrew S. Burrows, and Richard Fieldhouse, *British, French, and Chinese Nuclear Weapons* (1994).

David Irving, *The German Atomic Bomb* (1968, reprinted 1983), covers the German program in World War II, as does Thomas Powers, *Heisenberg's War* (1993, reissued 2000). John W. Dower, "'NI' and 'F': Japan's Wartime Atomic Bomb Research," in John W. Dower (ed.), *Japan in War and Peace* (1993), examines wartime Japanese work on the atomic bomb.

Avner Cohen, *Israel and the Bomb* (1998), provides a pathbreaking study of the domestic and international political context that shaped Israel's nuclear program; this should be supplemented by Seymour M. Hersh, *The Samson Option: Israel's Nuclear Arsenal and American Foreign Policy* (1991).

There is a growing literature about the Indian bomb: George Perkovich, *India's Nuclear Bomb: The Impact on Global Proliferation*, new ed. (2002); Itty Abraham, *The Making of the Indian Atomic Bomb* (1998); Ashley J. Tellis, *India's Emerging Nuclear Posture* (2001); and Raj Chengappa, *Weapons of Peace: The Secret Story of India's Quest to Be a Nuclear Power* (2000).

A well-founded history of the Pakistani bomb remains to be written. Gordon Corera, *Shopping for Bombs: Nuclear Proliferation, Global Insecurity, and the Rise and Fall of the A.Q. Khan Network* (2006), focuses on Abdul Qadeer Khan and his network.

The South African program is described by David Albright, "South Africa and the Affordable Bomb," *The Bulletin of the Atomic Scientists*, 50(4):37–47 (July/August 1994); and Peter Liberman, "The Rise and Fall of the South African Bomb," *International Security*, 26(2):45–86 (Fall 2001). Dismantlement plans are outlined in Waldo Stumpf, "South Africa's Nuclear Weapons Program: From Deterrence to Dismantlement," *Arms Control Today*, 25:3–8 (December 1995/January 1996), written by the chief executive of the Atomic Energy Corporation. J.W. de

Villiers, Roger Jardine, and Mitchell Reiss, "Why South Africa Gave Up the Bomb," *Foreign Affairs*, 72(5):98–109 (November/December 1993), explains the reasons.

David Albright and Kevin O'Neil (eds.), *Solving the North Korean Nuclear Puzzle* (2000), examines the fuel cycle and the agreement with the United States. Yoichi Funabashi, *The Peninsula Question: A Chronicle of the Second Korean Nuclear Crisis* (2007), concentrates on the events after October 2002.

Jeffrey T. Richelson, *Spying on the Bomb: American Nuclear Intelligence from Nazi Germany to Iran and North Korea* (2006), assesses Washington's efforts to monitor the nuclear weapons programs of foes and friends. Proliferation developments are monitored by the Carnegie Endowment for International Peace, which has published Joseph Cirincione, Jon B. Wolfsthal, and Miriam Rajkuma, *Deadly Arsenals* (2002), a comprehensive review. *Bulletin of the Atomic Scientists* (bimonthly) has followed the above topics since 1945 and should be consulted for current developments.

Samuel Glasstone and Philip J. Dolan (compilers and eds.), *The Effects of Nuclear Weapons*, 3rd ed. (1977, reprinted 1989), is a standard reference work.

NUCLEAR STRATEGY

Historical background to contemporary strategic thinking is found in Peter Paret (ed.), *Makers of Modern Strategy* (1986). An overall survey is John Baylis et al., *Strategy in the Contemporary World: An Introduction to Strategic Studies* (2002). Lawrence Freedman, *The Evolution of Nuclear Strategy*, 3rd ed. (2004), summarizes the history of thought on nuclear strategy. Fred Kaplan, *The Wizards of Armageddon* (1983), is a look at the thinkers and strategists themselves.

The classics of postwar strategic thinking include Bernard Brodie, *Strategy in the Missile Era* (1959); Herman Kahn, *On Thermonuclear War*, 2nd ed. (1961, reprinted 1978), and *On Escalation: Metaphors and Scenarios* (1965, reprinted 1986); and Thomas C. Schelling, *The Strategy of Conflict* (1960, reprinted 1980), and *Arms and Influence* (1966, reprinted 1976). Among later contributions, Edward N. Luttwak, *Strategy: The Logic of War and Peace*, 2nd ed. (2002), is a complex scholarly treatment of strategy as a system of thought; and Colin Gray, *Modern Strategy* (1999), provides a challenging critique of contemporary thinking.

Guides to theories of deterrence are found in Patrick M. Morgan, *Deterrence Now* (2003); and Lawrence Freedman, *Deterrence* (2004). Analyses of deterrence in practice include Alexander L. George and Richard Smoke, *Deterrence in American Foreign Policy: Theory and Practice* (1974). Paul Bracken, *The Command and Control of Nuclear Forces* (1983), is another authoritative treatment; and John J. Mearsheimer, *Conventional Deterrence* (1983), applies the deterrence theory to land warfare. An analysis of the strategic implications of recent conflicts is found in Rupert Smith, *The Utility of Force in the Modern World* (2006).

BIOLOGICAL WEAPONS

Barry R. Schneider, "Passive Defenses Against Chemical and Biological Attacks," chapter 5 in *Future War and Counterproliferation: U.S. Military Responses to NBC Proliferation Threats* (1999), pp. 79–116, summarizes chemical and biological warfare threats and possible passive defense countermeasures to neutralize such threats.

Malcolm Dando, *The New Biological Weapons: Threat, Proliferation, and Control* (2001), looks at the challenges caused by technical advances in the field of biology and the means to cope with the increasing threats of future biological weapons.

Frederick R. Sidell, Ernest T. Takafuji, and David R. Franz (eds.), *Medical Aspects of Chemical and Biological Warfare* (1997), is an excellent introduction to both the history and the medical aspects of biological warfare.

Joshua Lederberg (ed.), *Biological Weapons: Limiting the Threat* (1999), covers all aspects of biological warfare, including its history, arms control, Iraq's biological warfare program, the Soviet anthrax incident at Sverdlovsk, and bioterrorist issues.

Ken Alibek and Stephen Handleman, *Biohazard* (1999), is the best single book on the dimensions and details of the former Soviet biological warfare program by the top scientist (Alibek) in the program.

Sheldon H. Harris, *Factories of Death: Japanese Biological Warfare 1932–1945 and the American Cover-up*, rev. ed. (2002), is the best single history of the Japanese biological warfare program from the 1930s until the end of World War II.

CHEMICAL WEAPONS

Eric Croddy, *Chemical and Biological Warfare: A Comprehensive Survey for the Concerned Citizen* (2002), details the properties and evolution of chemical and biological weapons, as well as the historical efforts to impose arms control and disarmament limitations on their development, production, possession, and use. Albert Mauroni, *Chemical and Biological Warfare*, 2nd ed. (2007), is an excellent summary of chemical and biological warfare problems and solutions that also contains information on case studies, organizations, and further resources on the subject. Jonathan Tucker, *War of Nerves: Chemical Warfare from World War I to Al-Qaeda* (2006), is a unique set of historical case studies of chemical and biological terrorism, including lessons learned and motivational factors. Stephen F. Burgess and Helen E. Purkitt, *The Rollback of South Africa's Chemical and Biological Warfare Program* (2001), details Project Coast, the South African chemical and biological weapons program that started in 1981 and was finally terminated in 1994. Jonathan Tucker,

"The Yellow Rain Controversy: Lessons for Arms Control Compliance," *The Nonproliferation Review*, Spring 2001, is a comprehensive discussion of the history of the controversy over whether the Soviet Union and its Vietnamese and Laotian communist allies used mycotoxins against resistance forces in Laos and Cambodia in the 1970s.

ARMS CONTROL

Helpful sources on arms control include Steve Weber, *Cooperation and Discord in U.S.-Soviet Arms Control* (1991); Fen Osler Hampson, Harald von Riekhoff, and John Roper (eds.), *The Allies and Arms Control* (1992); Martin E. Goldstein, *Arms Control and Military Preparedness from Truman to Bush* (1993); Nancy W. Gallagher (ed.), *Arms Control: New Approaches to Theory and Policy* (1998); David B. Thomson, *A Guide to the Nuclear Arms Control Treaties* (2001); and Thomas Graham, Jr., *Disarmament Sketches: Three Decades of Arms Control and International Law* (2002).